'With an ageing population and inevitable that dementia – the ur stay, for the foreseeable future at more important that we learn to kindness and compassion. This book – so well researched and beautifully written – will be of significant value to the many who find themselves embarking, or continuing, on the journey that dementia demands. We all have a lot to learn from the lived experience, careful reflection and insights that Robin has documented.'

Phil Parker, Lead Nurse, National Prion Clinic, UCLH NHS Foundation Trust

'This is a book that will make you both laugh and cry with Robin's touching and truthful account of how he and his wife Shoko journeyed through her Alzheimer's. It's a love story not just about their marriage – and this shines through on every page – but also about how the real identity of the self retains its dignity and meaning grounded in the love of family, the wider community and above all in the love of God. It's a practical book that reflects on how to cope and how to find support as a carer, with a valuable message for people of all ages.'

Robin and Ursula Weekes, Emmanuel Church, Wimbledon

'With dementia diagnoses on the rise in the UK, the public and services will need to learn how to respond in better and more joined-up ways. It is too easy to mechanise the support and forget that there's a person inside. This story highlights the critical importance of combining clinical intervention, support work and good quality advice with compassion and kindness. While people do lose parts of themselves to dementia, they retain that which is common to us all: their feelings. We must never forget that people and families

living with dementia respond best to kindness and empathy.'
Rob Clarke, CEO, Age UK, Merton

'Robin manages to tell a personal and moving account of loneliness and loss, tempered by his faith and the love that he had for Shoko, and she for him. This book will be a very helpful resource for carers of loved ones with Alzheimer's, as it does not assume that Robin's experience is the same as others' or that "one size fits all" when it comes to caring. So he provides an excellent list of resources and raises a number of pertinent questions about future care. With 850,000 people living with dementia in the UK, along with their carers, these questions need urgent answers.'
Dr Tim Billington, former GP, Southampton

'My husband, a former surgeon and GP, was diagnosed with Alzheimer's Disease at the age of seventy-five, in the midst of an active, busy life. So I faced many of the challenges described here in my own life. I can identify with so much in this honest, vivid and very personal account. It will help others facing the same journey of adjustment and will enlighten those who want to understand more about dementia in all its varied presentations.'
Margaret Gould, former caregiver and advocate for those living with dementia

'This is a really thoughtful and honest read and an informative account of how it is to live with dementia. Every individual with dementia is different and every carer is different, but there are some common themes and experiences which we all share at one time or another. Robin's experiences were very much connected and influenced by his Christian faith while other couples and families gain strength through other channels. What comes through strongly is the need for appropriate support at the right time, whether physical or psychological or spiritual. The "Helpful Resources" section at the end adds to the value of the book.'

Margaret Dangoor, trustee of the Centre for Ageing Better, Carers UK and Crossroads (Richmond and Kingston upon Thames) and active in the dementia and carer community

'One family's journey living with dementia: how they learn to adapt and seek help from friends and healthcare professionals in order to cope with everyday life. Beautifully written, emotive and informative, this book is for anyone affected by dementia to read and gain insight from.'

Kim Barnes, community dementia nurse, Central London Community Healthcare NHS Trust

'The book describes with sensitivity and candour the journey that Robin and his children took in caring for his wife, Shoko, through the different stages of Alzheimer's – the confusion of not understanding the progression of the disease, especially in its early stages; frustration and tiredness from trying to respond to unpredictable behaviour; the assistance they needed to manage the unknowable length of time that it would last. There are details of helpful books, people, organisations and other resources. But more than anything else, this is a love story: in Robin's love for Shoko he learned to love more deeply, humbly and sacrificially, and in response, the effects of Alzheimer's could not extinguish the expression of Shoko's love for him.'

Dr Iain Aitken. professor of international public health

'A beautiful love story and honest account of a family navigating the uncertainties caused by dementia, written with such compassion, understanding and emotional intelligence. Through reflection and vulnerability, Robin is able to offer the reader valuable insight and practical advice through the different stages of the disease. A must-read for all those affected by dementia whether personally or professionally.'

Kim Smith, Dementia & End of Life Care Clinical lead, (Merton) Central London Community Healthcare NHS Trust

'When I last talked with Shoko, in a melée of people following the funeral of a friend, I found myself wondering, "What must it feel like to fail to recognise oneSELF?" In this very personal memoir, Robin Thomson shares some of what it was like: his slowness to discern/admit what was happening; his constant carefulness for Shoko's dignity; every day a new day, fresh-born from nowhere; learning from and with his children; his cold hands; having to go out and ring the doorbell again in order to be recognised. Distract, redirect, divert...

'An intercontinental marriage, full of surprises, some wonderful carers, remarkable patience, winsome honesty, precise and concise reflection. The book is a treasure, a love story, full of wisdom.'

Howard Peskett, author and theologian

LIVING WITH ALZHEIMER'S

A love story

Robin Thomson

instant apostle

First published in Great Britain in 2020

Instant Apostle
The Barn
1 Watford House Lane
Watford
Herts
WD17 1BJ

British Library Cataloguing-in-Publication Data

A catalogue record for this book is available from the British Library.

This book and all other Instant Apostle books are available from Instant Apostle:

Website: www.instantapostle.com

Email: info@instantapostle.com

ISBN 978-1-912726-19-6

Printed in Great Britain.

Contents

Introduction

In January 2012 my wife, Shoko, was diagnosed with Alzheimer's disease. We had no clue about what lay ahead. A few years later, when the disease actually took over our lives, we learned the hard way. We had been married nearly fifty years, living in twenty-three homes in India, the UK and Japan (where Shoko was born), bringing up our two children, sharing our life together. Now we went through discouragement and relentless pressure as her personality changed and she lost her capacity in many areas of life. What kept us going were the love and practical help of family and friends, and the remarkable friendship and support of the carers who visited us, backed up by health and social care professionals.

Even more remarkable was my growing awareness of Shoko's constant affection and love, despite the decline in her mental ability. It was a deeply spiritual journey.

This is *our* story: we know that each person's experience of Alzheimer's (or other forms of dementia) is different. But there are common questions. What can you do to help the person you are caring for and sustain yourself? What resources are available? That is what we began to discover.

This is written for other caregivers, families and friends who share the same pain and pressure, as well as hope and resources.

Attitudes are changing. But fear and incomprehension are still the most common responses to Alzheimer's. It truly is a fearsome and mysterious disease. But perhaps we can learn how to respond with love and more understanding.

The Story

1
The Wave Came Very Slowly

The tsunami struck Japan on 11th March 2011. With the rest of the world, we watched in horror. We were due to fly to Japan ten days later, but everybody there told us not to go.

Fortunately, we were able to cancel our flights and other bookings. But now there was a different problem. We had planned to have our home rewired while we were away. It would be very messy, so we needed to leave the house. We arranged to visit our son and family in Geneva and began to pack things away as much as possible. Shoko didn't seem interested and couldn't help much. 'How did you manage to do it all?' she asked me afterwards. It was quite out of character but I put it down to our advancing age (*'anno domini'*, as my father would have said) and thought no more about it.

We didn't realise that our own tsunami was about to strike. It started so gradually that we hardly noticed it at first. But within five years we would feel we were drowning in frustration, confusion and loss. The wave came very slowly, but it would be very deep.

For now it was just on the horizon. By the time we were able to go to Japan, in October that year, I could see that Shoko had lost her 'edge'. I needed to prompt her to make contacts with family and friends once we were there. And she had begun to repeat questions and comments, forgetting what she had just said. Her sister, who had not seen her for three years, noticed it at once and was concerned. Shoko was now eighty-one years old, but looking and functioning like someone ten years younger. She was in good general health, walking and cycling everywhere. We needed to find out what was happening to her.

When we got home we consulted our GP, who referred us to the consultant at the Memory Clinic. A very nice doctor came to give Shoko various tests. She could handle the mental exercises well but couldn't remember the names of the Queen or Prime Minister.

'It looks like Alzheimer's disease,' he said, and in January 2012 that was confirmed by a scan and further tests.

Alzheimer's. What did that mean? We were not quite sure. In fact, we knew very little.

My father had developed it twenty-five years earlier. The family got used to his regular repetitive questions and it was difficult to have a 'normal' conversation with him. But he seemed able to manage his life and was always gracious and courteous. So we just accepted it, though we did feel an increasing sense of loss. We tried to support my mother, though we probably didn't do enough. Three years later my father died of heart failure, before his Alzheimer's had progressed much further. We knew very little about his actual disease. At that time awareness generally was low. There must have been literature and resources available, but we didn't know about them.

So when Shoko received her diagnosis we had no real idea what lay ahead. We didn't realise that memory loss could impact almost all areas of her life. I couldn't imagine that one day she wouldn't recognise our neighbours and sometimes her own children. That she would lose her amazing skills in cooking and stop reading books. Or that she would sit upstairs spending hours just taking things out of drawers and putting them back in. I couldn't anticipate the crushing sense of helplessness that our family would feel as we watched her.

All that was still in the future, when the wave would crash over us.

For now our diagnosis seemed clear. The scan revealed 'minimal diffuse atrophy' but 'no evidence of significant underlying small vessel blood disease'.[1]

I clung to the word 'minimal' and hoped for the best. Our doctor explained that the scan indicated Alzheimer's disease, the most common form of dementia, and not vascular dementia, the second most common. (Vascular dementia is sometimes associated with diabetes; but although Shoko had diabetes, what she had was Alzheimer's disease.)

---

[1] Letter from Merton Community Mental Health Trust dated 13th February 2012 (scan dated 16th January 2012).

Later, as we were introduced to books and articles, we learned about the other, less common types of dementia – frontotemporal, Lewy body and several more.

We learned that 'dementia' was the umbrella term for this range of mental disorders. The World Health Organization (WHO) definition includes several aspects, which combine in different ways:

> Dementia is a syndrome – usually of a chronic or progressive nature – in which there is deterioration in cognitive function (i.e. the ability to process thought) beyond what might be expected from normal ageing. It affects memory, thinking, orientation, comprehension, calculation, learning capacity, language, and judgement … commonly accompanied … by deterioration in emotional control, social behaviour, or motivation.[2]

Mild Cognitive Impairment (MCI) is used to describe a condition in which there is memory loss, but no other signs of dementia. In some cases, MCI leads on to dementia.

Many dislike the term 'dementia' with its negative connotations and the resulting stigma. Most agree that it isn't the best word – but so far nobody has come up with a better one.

In Japanese the word was officially changed from *chiho,* meaning 'dementia', with the same connotation of

---

[2] www.who.int/news-room/fact-sheets/detail/dementia (accessed 2nd October 2019).

being 'out of your mind', to *ninchisho* – 'disease of cognition'.[3] Perhaps a change in English will come as we understand the condition more accurately and so think differently about the people affected.

Once we had the diagnosis, what should we do next? Our doctor and consultant were helpful in giving us the medical facts. But for practical advice they both referred us to the Alzheimer's Society, which had an office next door to the consultant. Their representative was kind, came to visit Shoko and offered us their services, mostly groups that we could attend.

The consultant had explained that there was no cure and no way of reversing the effects. But he suggested one of the drug treatments available to slow down the symptoms. Shoko started Aricept (Donepezil) but she found it gave her side effects – vivid dreams at night and tension in the daytime. So she stopped and we looked instead for herbal remedies. We found curcumin, based on the spice turmeric (the familiar *haldi* we knew from India), and Shoko began taking the tablets regularly. We hoped this would contain the symptoms. Our doctor was sympathetic to this but pointed out that the progress of the disease was inevitable.

We were not sure how to measure that progress. Was it just memory loss, thinking of my father's example? Shoko realised that she had a memory problem but that was all. We didn't discuss it much. We weren't sure whether the sessions at the Alzheimer's Society would be useful (there was one that interested Shoko, but it was for

---

[3] Sally Magnusson, *Where Memories Go* (London: Two Roads, 2014), p 78.

carers only). She didn't particularly want to attend a group with people who had lost their mental abilities.

Were we in 'denial'? Yes and no. We definitely realised this was serious, but we simply hoped the disease would not get any worse, and might even get better, particularly with the herbal medicine. As already mentioned, we knew very little beyond the symptoms of memory loss that we had seen in my father. Perhaps, subconsciously, we didn't want to explore further? But it was more that we just didn't know. Nobody recommended any books or further resources that might have given more insight into what was already happening or would lie ahead.

Books published more recently discuss in some depth how people may respond to their diagnosis, both the persons being diagnosed and their family and friends.[4] There are remarkable examples of persons living with Alzheimer's but still able to speak and write about their experiences.[5] When I read their stories (much later) I was amazed at the insights they gave, from the inside, into what we were just beginning to experience.

But unlike many of these people, though she had some realisation, Shoko didn't seem to be fully aware of what was happening to her. Seven years earlier she had had a stent put in for angina and following that began to take regular medication. That appeared to have slowed down her general awareness, and might have been part of the reason that she didn't seem troubled by her diagnosis (as far as I could tell – who really knew?).

---

[4] See the books mentioned in the Helpful Resources section.
[5] For example, Wendy Mitchell, *Somebody I Used to Know* (London: Bloomsbury, 2019).

A close friend told us his wife had the disease, around the same time as Shoko. When they had passed through London I had been struck by her blank expression and lack of engagement, though I didn't know her diagnosis at the time.

We definitely had some feeling of stigma – we didn't want to talk about it to outsiders. Shoko never liked to talk about any illness to others, and I just hoped they wouldn't notice anything. Our GP suggested, 'Say you have some memory loss – they will understand.' (But actually they didn't.)

We continued in hope and carried on with the curcumin tablets. We didn't know whether they were helping her brain, but they certainly helped her knees and other joints. They had been arthritic and painful sometimes but she had much less trouble with them now.

From time to time we would read or hear about claims of new medicines for Alzheimer's. We knew enough to take them with a large pinch of salt, or realise that even if they had potential, it might be many years away. I did try one 'treatment' from a website that involved mixing precise amounts of salad and fruit in careful combinations over two weeks. I parted with $35, partly reassured by one reviewer who said his money had been refunded when the treatment didn't work. These people must be honest, I thought. How stupid can you be? The salad diet did no harm, but it didn't do any good either. Later we learned that a possible approach to dealing with

Alzheimer's might include special diets, among many other factors.[6] Maybe – but it definitely wasn't this one.

Could we, should we, have done more at that time to prepare for the future? The advice we received later was to seek to live well and to take each moment and each day as it came. In a way, that is what we were doing, without a great deal of knowledge.

John Killick, who has worked with many people living with dementia, comments:

> Since dementia and non-dementia form a continuum, and aspects … like memory loss are so common, we should as far as possible abandon the idea of a distinct before-and-after so beloved of testers and give as many positive experiences to everyone as possible … it would certainly make for a happier population than the current set-up.[7]

Looking back, we might have done things differently. But probably he is right and the way we carried on was the best for us.

The wave was still coming very slowly.

---

[6] See, for example, Dale Bredesen, *The End of Alzheimer's* (London: Vermilion, 2017); Dean and Ayesha Sherzai, *The Alzheimer's Solution* (London: Simon & Schuster), 2017. For a survey of attempts to find the causes and possible cures for Alzheimer's/dementia, see Joseph Jebelli, *In Pursuit of Memory* (London: John Murray, 2018).

[7] John Killick, *Dementia Positive* (Edinburgh: Luath Press Limited, 2014), p 135.

2
Made in Japan

In 2013 Shoko spent time writing about her childhood and early years in Japan. She wrote in Japanese and we recorded a version in English.

Shoko Hirata was born into a 'loving and strict' family in Maebashi, a medium-sized city, just north of Tokyo. She was the middle of three sisters. Her father, Nakahiro Hirata, was a chemist who worked with his father, developing new processes for manufacturing Japanese paper. Grandfather was a prominent local politician, as well as a successful businessman, amateur artist and calligrapher. The house was often full of guests.

Shoko wrote:

> *My granny was born in Tokyo and was from [the] Kubo family. We were always looking forward for her mother's visit [my great-grandmother] as she brought us lots of special gifts from Tokyo. Our granny was very hard-working. She spent much time in her kitchen and produced lovely meals for us as*

*well as the guests who came. She also loved reading
and embroidery.*

*My mother's name was Takako. Her family
(Marubashi) owned a company in Isesaki [about ten
miles away] weaving kimono silk. It became very
popular and they were quite wealthy. I loved to visit
my grandmother there and all my cousins.*

This grandmother managed her large family and the
family business after her husband died at quite a young
age. Both grandmothers were strong and capable women.
Gunma Prefecture, where they lived, was said to be the
home of *karakaze, kakadenka* – 'strong winds, strong
women'.

*My father's hobby was playing 'Go'. It was a very
skilled game and he was the number one player in our
Gunma Prefecture. When we saw his picture in the
newspaper, how proud we were of him.*

*Our most sad experience was my mother suffered
from TB, which was incurable in those days. In spite
of her sickness she knitted sweaters for us three
children and told us lots of stories before we went to
sleep.*

Shoko vividly described the street where she and her
friends played every day. They came home from school,
had a snack and then ran out to play. There were no cars
in the street, only the sellers of *ramen* and other kinds of
noodles. At the corner was the sweet shop where they
spent their pocket money, and behind them, in the
distance, was the beautiful shape of Mount Akagi. They
played and played until they heard the familiar evening

song through the loudspeaker, inviting the children to return home together, like the birds to their nests. Soon it would get dark and the moon would come out. Then *'Abayo, mata ashita'* ('Bye, see you tomorrow') and off to their homes for supper.

But when Shoko was twelve, both her parents died in the same year, her mother in the spring (from TB) and her father in the autumn (from a heart attack connected with his asthma). It was a devastating blow. She and her two sisters were brought up by their grandparents. Shoko had to return from the very good boarding school where she had just started.

Japan was now at war and she and her friends were sent – secretly, by their school – to work in a munitions' factory, making paper balloons intended to carry toxic gas across the sea to America. Air raids began and the children walked to school with cotton pillows on their heads. The family dug an air raid shelter in the garden. In August 1945 Maebashi was bombed by the US Air Force and half of it was destroyed. A school friend was killed. It was just one day before the nuclear attack on Hiroshima and ten days before the war ended.

Shoko remembered vividly the emperor's broadcast to the nation. It was the first time most Japanese had heard his voice and many were in tears, standing up as he spoke and straining to understand his courtly language. As he concluded that they must 'bear the unbearable', some were not sure what it all meant. Had Japan won or lost? The reality soon became clear and the deprivation at this time was worse than during the conflict: the family never sat down to eat, but carried some peas or beans to suck on as they worked. Money was not much use: Granny took their mother's beautiful kimonos, given by her silk-weaving family, and exchanged them for handfuls of rice.

Life was not all bad. At this time Shoko was part of *'Etoile'*, a discussion group held in her cousin's bookshop. The members were mostly students from good universities. Two of the girls, from rich families, were communists, at that time illegal in Japan. They spent their time reading books and holding discussions. Shoko was the youngest and smallest member, affectionately nicknamed *'Run-chan'* because she was always running here and there, on errands for others.

In the midst of these good and bad experiences, she was struggling with the loss of her parents. An English missionary, Dorothy Parr (*'Parr Sensei'*), who lived opposite their house, had been a good friend of the family for some years, especially when her mother was ill. She continued her friendship and invited Shoko to their church. She was reluctant but her grandmother persuaded her to accept, in response to Dorothy's kindness. There Shoko found friendship and love. When she was sixteen she became a follower of Jesus. It was a turning point in her life.

After leaving school, Shoko worked as a Japanese language teacher and then seized an opportunity to work as a stenotypist in an office in Tokyo. She worked for a German company that imported heavy machinery to Japan. The small office team got on well with each other and with Mr Schmidt, their kindly German boss. They had quite a few perks, including free lunches and the opportunity to buy clothes and other goods on credit.

Moving to the big city was an adventure. Shoko recorded in her journal the concerts she attended, the films she saw and the books she read – from piano recitals to French films (with Jean Gabin) to English, French and Russian writers (in translation) to Japanese novels and essays.

They were good years. But she felt restless and wanted to do more in her life. When she was eighteen she had told God that she was willing to serve anywhere in the world. She began to save money and in 1959 she left Japan to study at Moody Bible Institute in Chicago – a 'courageous decision', as one of her cousins wrote later, 'because Japanese people could not go abroad easily in those days'. Her grandmother and two cousins waved her off in the ship from Yokohama. Friends met her in San Francisco and she travelled by train across to Chicago. 'Moody seemed like heaven,' Shoko wrote later. The staff and other students were kind and welcoming and she made life-long friends. During the term she helped in a local Japanese-speaking church, where she made more friends. In the summer vacation she followed a friend's introduction to an elderly lady in Seattle. Although Grace Armstrong had never met Shoko before, she looked after her like a daughter, found her a summer job and introduced her to her circle of friends.

After three years it was time to return to Japan, but a friend there advised her to get further qualifications so that she could teach at Japan Bible Seminary, of which he was the principal. So she stayed another year to earn some money and then crossed the Atlantic to study for two years at London Bible College (now London School of Theology). LBC was another place to learn and grow, and

Shoko made new and deep friendships with others who also wanted to serve in different parts of the world.

In September 1966 she returned to Japan on a French ship, *SS Laos*, sailing from Marseilles to Yokohama, in the crowded Economy Class (*'Classe Cabine'* sounded better in French). On board two Sri Lankan women told her about a young man called Robin, who had also studied theology. We met the next day. (They had told me, too, about the Japanese girl who had studied theology.)

I had just graduated from university and was on my way to India to teach at Hindustan Bible Institute in Madras (now Chennai). My family had a long connection with India as my parents had worked there as missionaries. My older sister, younger brother and I were all born in India and did our early schooling there. I now planned to spend two years in Madras and then return to the UK for further study and training.

Shoko and I found we had a lot in common. She had plenty of questions from her theological study and we had some lively discussions. In the next nine days we talked a lot, sat on deck studying the Bible or looking at the stars, watched the occasional films in the ship's dining room, and shopped for bargains in Aden. We also organised a Sunday 'church' service in the same dining room, along with an eccentric Indian preacher.

On 18th September we reached Bombay (now Mumbai), where I had to leave the ship. I was fascinated by this Japanese girl but I didn't quite realise what I felt about her. I wrote to my sister in London that this was definitely a 'platonic friendship'. After our first meeting Shoko wrote in her journal (which I only saw recently):

'He appeared to me a very sincere Christian boy. Brown hair, dark blue eyes (?) and quite tall.'

It was hard to say goodbye.

We began to exchange letters. Shoko wrote about her teaching as well as her work with Scripture Union, translating and editing Bible study notes. She worked long hours and longed for more people to work alongside her. I was busy starting my new role and relating back to India again. By May the following year I realised that I must write to express my love for her. But as we exchanged our responses I felt that it would not work out: Shoko was several years older than me (which I had never guessed when we met); there were differences of culture and language; I felt called to work in India, while she had trained to work in Japan.

She answered all my questions, firmly and graciously: 'Please forgive me, Robin, for writing so much. If I were a real Japanese girl I would never have done so.' But she accepted my decision and we thought we should not correspond any more.

But we did keep in touch, and in May 1968 she was sent to a conference in Singapore. (Her boss, who knew about our friendship, encouraged her to go.) Should she come across to Madras? Our letters crossed and she ventured again. We met once more and I asked her to marry me.

Shoko went back to Japan to tell her family and friends, and prepare to return to India. We were married in January 1969, in Madras.

3
'Our Mother Was an Adventurer'

After we got married, Shoko and I spent most of the next twenty years in India, in different parts of the country, with times of home assignment in the UK and Japan. We began in Madras, where I taught at Hindustan Bible Institute, training future church workers and pastors. Shoko kept an open home for colleagues and students, local friends and guests from many places, while also teaching Greek. She loved hospitality and developed her skills in cooking – Japanese, Indian, Chinese, Western. The students loved her smile and her cooking.

Madras had two seasons – 'hot' and 'hotter' – and it was humid almost all the time. That was tiring. But we enjoyed living there and made close friends. We tried to learn Tamil together (more difficult because almost all our work was in English). I made halting progress in Japanese, but never enough. Shoko was passionate about dogs and we rescued one from cruelty and then acquired a puppy of our own, Snoopy. Our daughter, Sarah, was born and lived her first year in Madras. Jonathan was born two years later while we were on home assignment in London.

I learned how adaptable and brave Shoko was. She was used to crowds, from Tokyo, but not to dirt and dust, which she hated. Yet she always preferred to travel by bus, when she could, rather than the taxis or autorickshaws which other expatriates used. And she moved house, uncomplainingly, many times.

Perhaps our biggest test came after we had visited Japan for the first time as a family. We returned to Madras to find that our home in an old bungalow just off the college campus had been systematically burgled. Everything except furniture had been taken. There was just one bundle, wrapped in a bedspread, which the thief had left behind in his haste, with our precious wedding album and a few other things.

We were devastated and Shoko found it the hardest – especially losing the children's toys, not to mention *everything* else. Friends were extremely kind and generous. But it was easy to become bitter and blame the local people. What moved Shoko most of all was a visit from a woman whom we scarcely knew, living in a small and poor house behind us. She brought a beautiful china teapot and cups. 'It melted my heart,' Shoko said.

After seven years we were transferred to New Delhi for administrative work in our mission and two years later back to teaching, at Union Biblical Seminary.

UBS was located in a small town called Yavatmal, right in the centre of India. After living in the big, cosmopolitan New Delhi, this was a huge culture shock for Shoko. We arrived at the end of the hot, dry summer, when very little grew. On the second day colleagues took us to see 'the shops'. Shoko's eager anticipation turned to dismay: the main grocery shop was smaller than our living room and the vegetable market had only potatoes, onions and some dried up *bhindi* (okra). Nothing else. How would she feed her family? How could she stay in this place? But how could she fail her husband and the mission leaders whom we had consulted before coming here? We had been preparing to come for almost two years and had turned down other possible openings. Shoko became depressed. She came out of it through the wise and understanding counsel and support of our mission leaders, and through her prayer and faith that God had not made a mistake in bringing us to Yavatmal: 'Miraculously, in the same kitchen where I had been in despair, I was now able to sing.'

From that kitchen Shoko entertained colleagues and students and started cooking classes for students' wives. They enjoyed learning to make noodles from scratch or to bake cakes in a home-made oven.

When the college relocated to the city of Pune (a more appropriate setting in an increasingly urbanised India), Shoko began to help in Scripture Union camps and Bible classes at the church. She rescued several more of India's stray dogs (her beloved Snoopy had been followed by another dog, Sophie). And on top of that she gave all her care and attention to looking after Sarah and Jonathan. Sending them off to boarding school, thirty hours away by train, was a very difficult experience. Shoko kept in touch with letters every week and we lived for the long winter holidays. Sarah and Jonathan grew up in India and went to school there until they were seventeen and fifteen respectively.

Later Sarah wrote her impressions of those years:

Our mother was an adventurer – independent, intrepid and determined.

Over twenty years in India she lived in three cities and a small town, moved house eighteen times, settled us into eight different schools, travelled up and down the country on her own, rescued dogs and gained [a large] scar from a bite on her wrist after intervening in a fight to save our own dog, Snoopy.

It can't have been easy, constantly travelling and moving and making new friends – but our mother excelled at it.

No bus was so packed full of people that she wouldn't attempt to get on, often to our dismay. No pickpocket was to be tolerated – once, on a particularly crowded bus journey, she discovered her purse had been stolen and made such a fuss that it found its way back to her, handed above heads from one end of the bus to the other.

No meat market awash with blood and buzzing with flies was too revolting to enter. She would go where many other mothers feared to tread, and as children we were proud of this fact.

In all of this, her great achievement was to ensure that we barely noticed the upheavals. Wherever we were, she would find something beautiful to make it feel like home – a hand-printed table cloth, cushions, a lamp.

She had a huge energy for cleaning, never travelling without soap or duster; fifteen minutes

*into a hot train journey she would have wiped down
our compartment and washed the loo.*

*And she could magic up incredible food at any
time of the day or night – a delicious picnic for every
outing, for every journey, no matter how short.*

This was how she expressed her love for us.

In 1988 the whole family returned to the UK, living for
three years at World's End in Chelsea. Shoko cycled
round that part of London, shopping for bargains in
Harrods, Peter Jones and other stores. She loved to pick
up beautiful china, kitchen ware and fabrics in her
favourite blue or pink and enjoyed the tablecloths,
curtains and cushion covers she had collected from India.
She entertained frequent guests, including family from
Japan and friends from India. She was active in the local
church and made many good friends. One of them
recalled how she and Shoko were together visiting in a
large building with flats: 'A workman came because the
lifts weren't working and they had to use the stairs. Shoko
said "let's have a race" to him and he was so touched by
her sense of fun that they did race up the stairs together.'

We went back to India for another two years in 1991.
We lived in a small flat with continual water problems. It
was hard in the unforgiving heat of summer, but Shoko
coped with her usual adaptability.

We returned to the UK in 1993 to live in Raynes Park.
To our surprise, after moving so often in the previous
twenty-four years, we stayed in one place for the next
twenty-five. It was a quiet neighbourhood, which our
children considered 'boring' after living in Chelsea. We
enjoyed fields and woods just across the road, where we

could walk with our dog, Chibi. We were closely involved in our local church and made good friends there, as well as among our neighbours. One of Shoko's great loves was watching the tennis championships at Wimbledon and she had several heroes among the men. During these years in London she was able to visit family and friends in Japan more often than before.

Shoko was a great letter writer, to friends around the world. Her letters included lively descriptions, practical advice and the occasional recipe. A younger colleague in India recalled:

> Some good advice when I arrived as a nervous rookie in Pune: 'Before you go anywhere pray that the Lord will make you a blessing to those you meet.' Her words have stayed with me and helped me through my life. Shoko was always full of practical loving.

In 2001 Sarah got married to Tom and their daughter, Sasha, was born in 2005. Becoming grandparents was a rich experience for us, and soon Shoko began to look after Sasha one day a week. She became known as 'Baba', a diminutive of the Japanese *Obāsan* ('Grandmother').

Jonathan married Elsa in 2005 and they lived abroad, in Paris, Beijing, Geneva and Tokyo, for his work with the Foreign Office. So we saw their children, Maya, Noé and Luca, less often, but they soon got to know and love 'Baba' as well. Her increasing illness didn't make a difference to their relationship with her.

4
Losing Things, One by One

In the first year after Shoko's diagnosis, life continued much as normal. She could still manage day-to-day activities – looking after the house, cooking, sewing, writing letters, cycling here and there. When her cousin sent us a book he had edited, with the history of her mother's family and their successful silk-weaving business, she wrote in all the names of her aunts and uncles and cousins in English. She continued to compile photos for her series of family albums, going back to the beginning of our marriage.

But she lacked an overall framework.

'What day of the week is it today?'

If I said 'Sunday' or 'Monday' she knew what that meant and what activities were connected with it. But she could never remember that Monday night was the time to put the rubbish out for collection. By Saturday she would want to put it out. I found this an irritation: why couldn't she remember the correct date?

At the same time, I did begin to realise what an extraordinary thing memory is. When you start the morning not knowing what day it is, not remembering what happened yesterday, not quite sure what happens next, each day is a succession of new experiences. We received a book called *Helps to Memory* from the Alzheimer's Society. It had useful tips on how to strengthen memory by writing things down, making lists and so on. But already Shoko was unable to do any of that. We had a sign about the rubbish day on the fridge. I would point to it, but it had no relevance for her: she had already passed that stage.

'Until you start losing your memory, you take it for granted.'[8] But when it starts going, you can't plan, you can't look forward to things, you can't keep track of things you are doing. You lose the security of knowing what has just happened and the assurance that it will continue.

I had begun to work part-time and could work from home, which meant that my hours were flexible. We tried to take alternate days when we would do things together, travelling in London, going shopping or to museums and galleries. Sarah was living with her husband, Tom, not far away in Tooting. We saw them often and Shoko continued to look after our granddaughter, Sasha, on Tuesdays. She would pick her up from school and bring her home to play and have supper. I would then take her back to her parents in Tooting. Jonathan and Elsa were living abroad, but we saw them from time to time as well. They were all very supportive, as we watched for signs of

---

[8] Jude Wilton, *Can I Tell You About Dementia? A Guide for Family, Friends and Carers* (London: Jessica Kingsley Publishers, 2013), p 15. See also Magnusson, *Where Memories Go*, pp 201-202.

change. They too had earlier experienced my father's illness.

Shoko's memory wasn't very good. But it didn't seem to be getting worse. Maybe, I thought, the herbal medicine was helping her.

But something else was happening. Shoko began to be concerned that things were missing from the house. We had a lodger who shared the downstairs bathroom and a passage where we stored things. Shoko was convinced that the lid of a container had been opened and rice was being taken from it. I didn't think so, reassured her, and didn't take it too seriously. But a few weeks later she saw that a gold chain and brooch were missing from the bedroom and couldn't be found anywhere. This led to greater tension and in the end we decided that we would have to ask our lodger to leave. It was difficult for the lodger, and a very unhappy time for us. Shoko was convinced that things had been stolen. She insisted that we call the police. (They came, listened carefully and advised us that pressing charges could create a very difficult situation.) I didn't understand what was happening and found it hard to handle.

Shoko continued to worry that things were going missing. Again and again, she would count the cushions in the sitting room, the mugs hanging in the kitchen, the cutlery and plates in the drawers and cupboards. We made lists of everything and put them in prominent places. Shoko began to move things and hide them so they wouldn't be taken.

She worried about any cup or mug that seemed near the edge of the table and would move it away. She insisted on keeping the dining room cupboard with her best china locked. We kept the key in a small box in a drawer. She couldn't always remember where it was, and then she would find it and insist that we needed to move it to a safer place. ('But where?' I thought. 'You will forget again…') So we argued – quite fiercely at one point – over where to keep the key.

I found all this tiresome, and often became irritable. I tried to reason with her that everything was safe. The house was locked. The lodger had gone and we had changed the locks. Nobody could get in to take things. She was not convinced.

I knew that her behaviour was not normal. But I didn't really connect all this with Alzheimer's, because I thought that was primarily about memory loss. That was what we had observed with my father. And Shoko seemed reasonably stable in that regard.

So I was just irritated. And in fact I was really troubled by what was happening. Some mornings I lay in bed, wondering how to get up and face the day. I felt so helpless. But I thought that if I could *explain* things better, Shoko would understand. So I did my best to reason with her, without great success. Our son, Jonathan, told me there was no point in reasoning, but I didn't see it that way at the time. A close friend gave a lot of help and advice over the missing objects and dealing with the police, but didn't make a connection either with Alzheimer's. So we just struggled on.

What I learned later might have helped me to respond better. Books that I read afterwards explained how Alzheimer's affects different parts of the brain:

- Cognitive – difficulty with memory, losing things, storing things in odd places to keep them safe.

- Emotional – becoming agitated about small things, being suspicious or paranoid, getting impatient, for example about waiting in line. Shoko became very restless when we reached the supermarket checkout; she didn't want to wait.

- Functional – unable to plan, losing skills like sewing or cooking.[9]

Shoko's concerns and worries were completely consistent with the changes that were taking place in her brain. Reasoning with her was not necessarily the right response, because she wasn't being unreasonable or difficult. If I had understood this, could I have been more understanding and less stressed?

Other changes were taking place, step by step. The pattern of our life was being altered.

Shoko loved her sewing machine and could do (almost) anything with it. But one day she looked at it and couldn't remember the sequence to set it up. I couldn't do it without carefully studying the manual, so wasn't much help. She didn't open it again.

She was still cooking, but when it came to making her famous apple pie or Victoria sponge cake, I needed to do

---

[9] Simon Atkins, *First Steps to Living With Dementia* (Oxford: Lion Hudson, 2013), p 22; see also Wilton, *Can I Tell You About Dementia?*, p 17. Paraphrased.

all the measuring and eventually the whole thing (she still rolled the pastry and did the icing, for a while).

When we had guests, it became difficult for Shoko to plan and organise so I took charge and did most of the work, with all my limitations in the kitchen. Shoko wanted to help and advise, but would get confused. I should have been encouraging her to help and keeping her involved, as all the books I later read advised. But that wasn't easy to do, especially in the kitchen. In my controlling way, I wanted her to sit quietly at the table. 'Just let me get on with it,' I said. I didn't realise how different it would be when she really did sit quietly, in the years ahead.

We were experiencing the gradual loss of function of different parts of the brain, particularly the ability to plan and execute, along with certain skills.

One by one, she was losing them.

5
Closing Doors

Despite all that Shoko was gradually losing, our life still continued more or less normally. In September 2013 Tom and Sarah moved with Sasha to Barcelona, where Sarah joined the regional office of WHO. They were concerned about leaving us but we assured them that we were fine, though we would miss them greatly.

We kept what was happening to ourselves. From the outside nobody would have noticed any change, beyond our immediate family and close friends. (The family did notice and sometimes felt they needed to 'cover up' lapses in conversation or unusual behaviour, as Jonathan told me afterwards.)

Later we learned that the symptoms of Alzheimer's 'can be stable for up to five years'.[10]

But the wave was steadily advancing.

We were still going out as usual, by train or bus, enjoying the liberty of our Freedom Passes. Shoko's sense of direction had never been good, but she knew central

---

[10] Atkins, *First Steps to Living with Dementia*, p 11.

London well and we could arrange to meet at a straightforward spot, for example the ticket barrier on Platform 1 at Waterloo Station. But then a series of incidents brought an end to that.

Shoko had never been comfortable with a mobile phone. Early in 2013 we bought one with a simple display and she agreed to carry it. I phoned her to try it out, as she was going by bus to pick up Sasha from school. She answered, which was great – but as a result she missed her bus stop and got lost. A few minutes later the school phoned to say that nobody had come for Sasha. Then I got a call from another school to say that Shoko had arrived there. I had to go quickly to pick up Sasha and walk with her to the other school, where Shoko was waiting, not quite sure what had happened. We couldn't really use the mobile phone after that. And I began to pick up Sasha in Shoko's place.

Another day as we returned home she stopped to go the ladies' at the station, while I waited for her in the waiting room. After five minutes I began to look for her but she was not in the station. Somehow she had gone past me and was nowhere to be seen. And I was holding her handbag with her house keys. As I stood outside the station, peering at the bus stop and looking in the shops, our neighbour's car pulled up. He told me that Shoko was at their home. She had met one of our friends and they were waiting in our neighbour's house. He had very kindly come to tell me. What a relief: but what a worry as well. Would she get lost again?

A few weeks later I asked her to wait in the busy concourse at Wimbledon station, while I went outside to check something. When I came back, after just two minutes, she was no longer there and I had to search to find her. She had been confused and was anxiously looking for me. I realised I couldn't leave her on her own anywhere outside the home.

The following week Jonathan was visiting and we decided to go out to a restaurant in Tooting. I waited for Shoko and Jonathan at our station, just seven minutes' walk from the house. From there we would go together to Tooting. I meant to tell Jonathan not to let her out of his sight for a moment, but I didn't. A few minutes later he met me at the station – alone. A bus had arrived as they were walking past the bus stop, and Shoko had jumped on, saying she would get down at the next stop. But she didn't.

Where had she gone? Had she gone on to the restaurant (which would mean changing buses at Wimbledon)? We drove around looking for her, then went home, in case she would phone us there. We waited an hour, and had just phoned the police when amazingly she turned up. She had gone all the way to the restaurant and been puzzled not to find us there. Somehow she had managed to get the right bus to bring her back home.

I was very tense and stressed, but of course Shoko had no idea why. Jonathan thought I was cross with her. 'It wasn't her fault,' he kept saying. I wasn't cross with her, but with myself, for allowing this to happen. But it would have been hard for an observer to tell the difference. And I was also frustrated – and angry – that our situation had come to this.

Later Jonathan told me how sad he had felt, seeing his mother's loss of capacity and my inability to handle it well. He felt powerless and frustrated too.

Our life was changing, and not for the better, it seemed.

In 2013-14 we had travelled a lot, visiting Sarah and Jonathan and also going to India and Japan, where we enjoyed time with family and friends. However, it became harder and harder to leave the house. Shoko was worried that it wouldn't be safe. She also found it increasingly difficult to plan what to take and to pack her things. Setting out on a journey became more and more stressful, for both of us.

So in 2015 we only went away once, for a few days. The following year we made short visits to Tokyo and Barcelona. Shoko felt very unwilling to travel, but agreed to do what I suggested. Both times, as soon as we arrived, she was unsettled and wanted to go home. 'We can get a bus from here or go by the Underground,' she said. We all tried to explain why that wasn't possible, but she wasn't listening. With great difficulty we persuaded her to stay for a bit, and eventually she settled and we had good times with the family. But both times we had to change our flights and come home early. It was only later that I understood that she had thought she was still in London, and of course preferred to go home for the night.

After these two experiences I realised that we wouldn't be travelling anywhere again. It was another door closing on us.

I tried to go out and do things together on alternate days, but as 2016 went on I found that the pattern didn't work. I needed to be available any time, whenever Shoko felt like going out or doing something different.

In September we went to my cousin Janet's birthday party. Our extended family, who had not seen Shoko for a year or more, were shocked at how different she was. She greeted them all with her lovely smile but didn't really recognise them. But she went to the kitchen to help, as she had always done. Knowing how Shoko loved to help, Janet gave her a dish to take through. Shoko reached the kitchen door and then stopped. 'What did you ask me to do?' she said. Janet explained once more and the same thing happened again.

As I talked to another cousin there, I told him that I was still able to go out and leave Shoko at home, where she was contented and I had no worries about her being there on her own. He was relieved to hear it. 'You would find it very difficult otherwise,' he said.

But in fact it was around this time that I realised how much things had changed. Shoko was no longer able to initiate her own activities or plan what she would do each day. She couldn't finish things on her own. She stopped playing the piano. She was often confused about what was happening or who was in the house. When the family came to stay at Christmas, as usual, she was puzzled to see them in the kitchen or dining room.

In short, she was no longer able to manage daily life. She needed me to be with her, and was very dependent on me.

Suddenly Alzheimer's had begun to bite.

6

Into the World of Alzheimer's

By January 2017 we knew we had entered the shadowy, twilight world of full-blown Alzheimer's. Here nothing is quite what it seems and everything is unpredictable, both for the person with the disease and for those around them.

Shoko had made the transition *from* being able to manage daily life, though without a proper framework ('What day is it today?') and being sometimes eccentric, forgetful or overanxious, *to* becoming unpredictable, not really in control of her thoughts and actions, often confused, and increasingly dependent on others and especially on me.

It was the unpredictability that I found most difficult:

- How will we occupy this day?

- Will she eat lunch/supper?

- Will she be willing to go out, or will she resist?

- When we get home will she be confused and not want to go in?

- If somebody comes to the house will she recognise them and engage with them?

- Will she recognise me?

- At night will she go to bed and sleep? Will I be able to sleep…? (This became the big one, as I found later.)

And the dependence. I needed to be around all the time. Shoko had started calling me *'Otōsan'* ('Papa' – quite common for Japanese wives to call their husbands). So she would call out: *'Otōsan,* where are you?' Then again: *'Otōsan!' 'OtōōōSAN!'*

I would drop whatever I was doing, not always willingly.

I had been comfortable going out, leaving Shoko at home, but now I didn't feel I could leave Shoko on her own. I wasn't even sure if I could leave her with somebody else there. She seemed to be worried if I wasn't around.

By now Shoko was speaking much more Japanese. That was good for improving my limited understanding of the language, but sometimes frustrating if I didn't fully understand. She would not be able to translate what she had said. So I needed my little dictionary beside me. Sometimes she was unable to remember or repeat what she had just said. Often she couldn't finish a sentence, in Japanese or English.

Shoko had already been doing less in the kitchen. Now she stopped altogether, apart from clearing and washing dishes sometimes. She was happy to sit at the table and have her meals brought to her. That was what I had foolishly wished for earlier, when she would intervene in my culinary efforts. Now when it happened I found it very sad.

For several months Shoko had had pain in her back and hip. Walking became difficult and physiotherapy wasn't helping much. So opportunities to go out became very limited. We couldn't go for our usual walks, and getting to the station or even the bus stop was difficult. So no more travel round London or shopping in Kingston. Finding things to occupy ourselves became a challenge.

In the mornings Shoko would happily sit at the table after breakfast, looking at a magazine or photo album, for half an hour, maybe an hour, sometimes more, while I went upstairs and worked at my desk (there were always emails to read and send). She might then go to the kitchen and wash the dishes (though not always sure where to put them away). Later we would go out in the car, sometimes for physiotherapy or other errands. After lunch I would wonder how to occupy her. Perhaps we could play a game with cards or dominoes, or we could sing. I learned several Japanese songs around this time, in addition to the hymns which we both knew. We enjoyed singing together. Around 5pm we would go to our local supermarket. It was big and so walking around gave some exercise. Sometimes we would drive a bit more in the car. Then we came home and ate once again. Shoko would get ready for bed, which could take a while as she had no real plan to 'go to bed'.

Around this time she began going repeatedly to the toilet. Our GP thought it might be an 'irritable bladder'. He offered to prescribe pills but they might make her restless or sleepy or have other side effects, so she didn't take them. Quite soon it was evident that there was no physical need; it had become a nervous habit or syndrome.

She would say, 'I need to go to *oteārai*' (Japanese for 'the toilet' or 'the loo') or just '*oteārai*' and off she would go. Before doing anything or going anywhere she needed *oteārai*. If somebody came to the house and she was a bit nervous or restless she would disappear to *oteārai*.

It was easy for her to become stressed or anxious. A close friend had invited us for lunch. As we were preparing to leave, I happened to mention another person who had let somebody down. There was no connection, but Shoko thought this was our friend and immediately refused to go. 'How can we visit such an unreliable person?' she said.

I had to phone our friend and tell her that we couldn't come. She was very understanding and we rearranged the visit.

Early in the year we went to lunch with another good friend, Shona. We enjoyed our time there, as always. But as we were leaving she told me, 'You have to find support. You need to build up a team. Otherwise you can't manage.'

Shona realised that we had reached a new stage in Shoko's illness. From her experience with others she understood the new pressures that I was facing and knew that it could only increase. Later she said that she thought I looked terrible! I was not aware of our need in the same way, but realised that she was, of course, right.

Up to now I had felt I could manage, as I had done at times in the past, when Shoko had been ill or recovering from surgery. Now it was different. I couldn't do it on my own.

The next day another friend, Dick, was in touch. His parents had both lived into their nineties and had needed care in their final years. So he had experience of having to find carers to look after their physical needs (but not Alzheimer's). Dick told me the same thing as Shona: 'You need to find support. You must build your team.'

Around the same time a friend of Sarah introduced her to Margaret Dangoor, a carer with many years' experience, active in the dementia and carer community and chair of a local peer support group. She also had links with an excellent day care centre in a neighbouring borough. I wrote to Margaret and she replied at once, giving a lot of practical advice and recommending a person whom I could contact. This was Lynn James of a local care agency called Home Instead. Somebody else had mentioned her so I contacted Lynn at once. She agreed to come the following week to talk about options for providing a carer.

The day after we spoke it suddenly became even more urgent.

Daytimes had become a challenge, but Shoko still went to bed and slept each night. But on 24th January, she didn't go to bed. She said she needed to eat more and went downstairs to eat. Then she started her rounds in the toilet and bathroom and putting on face cream once again. Then she wanted to stay downstairs, to tidy up in the dining room, sort through her handbag, move things from one place to the other, anything except go to bed.

I didn't know what to do. I became more and more frustrated. Finally I gave her one of the sleeping tablets that she occasionally used, and waited. In the end, as she sat at the table she became sleepy and I was able to help her go upstairs and into bed. It was 1.45 in the morning.

Two nights later the same thing happened. This time I thought that I would go to bed and leave her to it. But she came into the bedroom and turned on the light. I got out of bed and we continued the circuit. She was not interested in going to sleep. I tried once again to lie down, this time in the spare room. I closed the door but Shoko came in, looking for me. Finally with the help once again of a tablet, she became drowsy and I was able to help her into bed. This time it was 5.45am.

The next morning I was exhausted and at my wits' end. What was I going to do? How could we continue in this way?

Now the wave had come crashing over us.

I phoned Lynn again and asked her to come urgently.

7
Carers

When we came back from India in 1993 Shoko had looked for work that she could do. A friend introduced her to a care agency and she began working several hours a week as a carer. She cycled (or sometimes drove) to people's homes to help them with meals or getting ready for bed, or other things that they needed. She enjoyed the work and was of course very good at it. Through it she felt she was learning a lot about how older English people lived.

She also helped look after Dorothy Parr, the missionary who had befriended her in childhood, when Dorothy finally returned to the UK. Shoko would visit her regularly in Bournemouth and spend a day with her, until she died aged ninety-seven.

So Shoko was a great carer of others. Sarah remembered her mother's commitment:

> *Our mother wanted people to do their best. She always tried to do the best she could and she wanted us to do the same, which I'm sorry to say I often resisted.*

> *If she committed to do something, she would throw herself into it – showing up to teach Greek in spite of heavy snow in Tokyo (disappointing her students, who were hoping for the day off); cooking curry for the whole of the church at St John's in Chelsea; passing her driving test – fourth time lucky aged sixty-five; and working as a carer for older people at a time when she was well past conventional retirement age herself.*
>
> *We wonder if she ever thought she would need the same sort of care herself.*

Now we did need carers ourselves. But what would they do, and would Shoko welcome them? She had no physical needs and did not see the need for anybody to come and help her. She also liked her own space and had never been really comfortable to have others in the house all the time.

We had been recommended a lady who was good at cleaning and had also been a carer for somebody else's mother. She came and was pleasant and cheerful. She spring-cleaned the whole house, which was great. And she was keen to do other work as well. But each time she offered to do something, Shoko told her she didn't need her help, she could do it by herself quite well. I wondered if there was a way in which they could do things together, to give me some space. But it didn't work out.

Would Lynn be able to find a more suitable person? She came in response to my urgent phone call. It was very helpful to talk to her and she promised to find the right carer to give companionship to Shoko. Perhaps somebody who could do some cooking with her, she suggested, maybe prepare an evening meal, and give me some time off. Soon after she brought a young Korean lady called Yuna whom she thought would be the right person. Yuna could spend time with Shoko, and they could cook together. As we talked, Yuna sat quietly at the other side of the table and I thought, 'This isn't going to work. She won't be able to do things with Shoko in the kitchen.'

After Yuna's visit, I wrote to my sister:

> *The main challenge, I think, will be for Shoko to realise why we are asking her to come ... when I explained that we were asking for some help with housework, etc, as well as perhaps teaching some cooking to Yuna, she wasn't very convinced. She said she would prefer not to have people around.*

The next day Yuna came on her own and the three of us sat and talked. Yuna had visited Japan and loved it. We soon began to talk about *sushi* and Shoko explained how to make it.

'We can make *sushi* together when I come next week,' said Yuna. And that is exactly what they did. The following visit they also made *tempura* together.

Yuna was good at stimulating Shoko. She asked her questions about her life and never seemed tired of talking with her. She also knew many of the songs that Shoko liked to sing from her hymn book. With her encouragement Shoko began to play the piano again, with Yuna singing along with her. Shoko was not quite sure about Yuna when she first came, but slowly became more and more at ease with her, while Yuna commented that she experienced unusual warmth and love from Shoko.

I was so grateful for this match. But I knew that we could not rely on Yuna alone. So we tried to find some other carers. It was a challenge to find the right person who could sit with Shoko and occupy her appropriately, as she didn't feel she needed any 'help'. None of them had quite the same rapport as Yuna so we didn't continue with them. One was very anxious to help but didn't quite click with Shoko. As she was leaving, she said, 'I'll see you next Tuesday.' Shoko replied, 'I don't think I'll be in that day.'

One of our friends from church, Jane Ann, phoned to say that she would be happy to come and visit Shoko. They had tea together and talked about dogs, or played games that Jane Ann brought from her role as an infant teacher. Shoko enjoyed it and I was able to go upstairs and clear some of my letters and other things.

Jane Ann came each week. My sister Elspeth also volunteered to come, as did Adela, Sarah's mother-in-law. They all came very willingly and spent time with Shoko, chatting, talking about dogs, looking at magazines, or playing songs on the computer. Two other friends, Clare and Yuko, came as well. Yuko brought delicious Japanese food and sang Japanese songs with Shoko.

This meant that I was able to go out and do things that I needed to do. I discovered that the local library was a good place to sit, with good internet access. Other friends phoned or emailed to keep in touch.

I felt I had some breathing space. But there was still a lot of the week left. Was there a way of getting more joined-up support?

8
Joined-up Support?

We were looking for more support. We contacted the Alzheimer's Society again and attended one of the drop-in sessions. People were friendly and I had a good talk with one of the staff. But Shoko was not particularly engaged. Some of the participants were enjoying puzzles or colouring but that didn't interest Shoko, and she passed the colouring page to me to do. It was quite a long way to travel and so we didn't continue.

The society sent their support worker to visit us. He gave very useful information about resources, including help with finance, council support, Blue Badge facilities, Attendance Allowance and more. This was extremely helpful for us as we followed up his suggestions.

We visited another drop-in centre closer to home. I thought that Shoko had really enjoyed it as she talked animatedly with several people. But when we went the following week she firmly refused to get out of the car and go in. I couldn't work out why. We did attend the monthly café run locally by the Alzheimer's Society. It was pleasant and Shoko enjoyed the first session, when they had a talented singer. But she didn't engage much with the other people there.

'What about your local day care centre?' a friend suggested. 'That would be really good for Shoko and it would give you time at home as well.' It was conveniently located and Shoko went there for three sessions, just two hours at a time to start with. The staff were friendly and caring and she seemed all right when I left her there, though she cried when I came to collect her. She didn't say anything the first two times but after the third time she told me it was too noisy and she didn't want to go back. Perhaps there was more activity than she wanted, or she just felt disorientated? I couldn't really find out but accepted that it wasn't working.

We continued looking around for any ways of support. I wrote to my sister again:

> *What about communal supported living (for both of us)? The advantage would be support from others. But it would be a huge upheaval. Again I'm not sure whether that would be helpful at this stage. But should we be exploring?*
>
> *Carers. This is the route we have begun and it's still early days to get the full benefit … Is there a way to get help in the evenings or at night? What would that look like? Night care is expensive – non-waking £180 / waking £250. Quite apart from the cost, what would be the value?*
>
> *There are some organisations offering respite care for a few hours, or longer.*
>
> *Day centre – the local one didn't quite suit … We have yet to arrange to visit the one a bit further away*

(for which we are in any case only on the waiting list).

One possibility which seemed most attractive to me at this time was to find a live-in carer. The family had decided together that we wanted Shoko to be at home, where she was comfortable and we could be with her. But I felt I needed more support for that. Live-in care might be a good option – sharing the task, not just for a few hours a day, but with somebody who would be there all the time. On the other hand, there was a disadvantage: somebody would be there all the time.

I thought seriously about this for several weeks and found some good possibilities. But as I thought more, I realised that as Shoko didn't need physical help, we didn't really need this type of care. I also didn't want to lose Yuna's help. She had become a good friend and support to Shoko.

So we decided to extend Yuna's time to four hours, three afternoons a week.

At the same time we looked for more helpers and found another one from Home Instead as well as a third person from Age UK. They both fitted in well and made good friends with Shoko. Sun Jin could speak Japanese as she had studied in Japan, and that was a great asset. Casey was only eighteen but very mature and Shoko reminded her of her grandmother, who had also had dementia. Another helper, Elizabeth, came for a while to fill one of the gaps.

Overall, it seemed that staying in her own surroundings at home, with one-to-one times with carers or friends, was the most enjoyable for Shoko.

The one exception was visiting Wimbledon Physiotherapy.

Shoko's back and hip had continued to give trouble. The physiotherapist arranged by our GP diagnosed it as bursitis but she didn't respond to the occasional physio sessions. They gave her exercises to do at home but she didn't understand and I wasn't able to motivate her. We arranged some sessions at Wimbledon Physiotherapy, hoping that at least she could do some of the needed exercises each time. We got much more than that.

Christine at reception greeted us warmly and Antonia, our physio, related to Shoko very personally. She began with gentle stretching and massage, going at her pace. Then they started throwing a ball to each other – and singing! Shoko loved singing and she especially loved her old Japanese songs. Antonia quickly picked up two favourites and they were off. Later Antonia found herself singing those songs at home, and the team at Wimbledon Physiotherapy enjoyed hearing them too.

Within a few weeks the hip problem was much better. Unfortunately, at that time Shoko got knocked over accidentally and had a compressed fracture in her back. Walking became difficult again. So we continued our sessions.

They became a highlight of our week. Antonia came right down to Shoko's level (literally – she was tall and Shoko was small). They smiled and laughed together and Shoko responded with her own affectionate personality. Some days she was tired and not really interested. Most days she loved it. Either way, Antonia was the same, always smiling and playing along with her.

Our sessions were not just exercise – though that was really valuable. They became outings to enjoy with a friend. Shoko also loved meeting the rest of the team and greeting the other clients, sometimes singing them a song, which both surprised and cheered them.

We were beginning to get into a pattern that could continue. We had a helpful visit from another charity, Carers Support Merton. They listened carefully to what we had been doing, felt that we were on the right lines, and introduced us to their support activities as well as other possible resources that we had not known about.

But we still felt very much on our own, searching here and there for what we could find. There was no person to whom we could turn for authoritative and practical advice – until we met the community dementia nurse, Phil Parker.

The Alzheimer's Society support worker put us in touch with him. Phil came to visit us and immediately developed a relationship both with Shoko and with me. He was warm and engaging. He was also a professional who could give us sound medical advice. So he combined both the medical and the personal, which was what we needed. He was always available by phone or email and responded promptly.

Phil offered to enrol Shoko in the new course that he was teaching called Cognitive Stimulation Therapy. This was considered to be as effective as medication, in some cases, to reverse the decline in cognitive ability. It ran for eight sessions, at the Alzheimer's Society centre. There was a small group of seven or eight other people, those with Alzheimer's and their carers. Phil and his colleagues led the group with great friendliness and warmth, engaging personally with each of the people there. Shoko was not able to follow some of the exercises and discussions, but she responded to the warmth and personal friendship of the leaders, as well as the others in the group.

At the end Phil came home to give Shoko a post-test to check whether there had been any cognitive development. Shoko greeted him and pointed to the hymn book she was looking at.

'Let's sing this together,' she said.

Phil joined in with two verses of 'What a Friend We Have in Jesus'.[11] He told us he had enjoyed singing in his church choir. Then he tried to start the test.

'Shoko, could you draw a clock for me here, please?'

Shoko was not very sure how to draw a clock and she wanted to sing. We sang another verse.

'Now can you tell me… '

'Let's go on singing,' Shoko replied, pulling his hand to take the hymn book again.

Phil knew when he was defeated and gave up the test.

He realised that Shoko had not made much progress in terms of cognitive development, but she had enjoyed the warm relationships.

And we knew we could count on Phil to answer our questions and point us to any resources on offer. This was exactly the joined-up support – the combination of medical and social care – that we had been looking for.

---

[11] Joseph Scriven, 1819–86.

9
Three Solid Pillars

After the two bad nights in January I didn't know what to do. I had started to build support through the network of carers and friends. But that didn't necessarily help with Shoko's sleep. And that was about to become even more difficult. A week later she woke up on two nights at around 2am. She opened cupboards and drawers and began to get dressed. She couldn't realise it was the middle of the night. I was in despair.

I needed some timely and very solid support, and I found it.

Remarkably, I had just renewed contact with an old friend, Tim Billington, a retired GP in Southampton. We had not met for more than forty years but had kept in touch through annual letters and mutual friends. Now we had unexpectedly connected through a completely unrelated project. I mentioned Shoko's illness and he told me that he had been helping some friends in exactly the same situation. So I asked him what to do about this sleep problem.

Tim's advice was very direct.

'Unless you can sleep, you won't be able to look after Shoko. So she needs to sleep and we need to find the best ways to help her with that.'

We talked through different ways of helping her to relax and settle, and how she could sleep through. Tim felt we should not hesitate to use medication, if needed, as that would be in our best interests, so that Shoko would be comfortable and I would be able to support her. In consultation with Tim, and with our GP's help, we worked out a combination that enabled Shoko to settle and also to sleep through the night. She began to sleep in the spare room, where it seemed easier to settle and she didn't have cupboards and drawers of clothes to distract her if she woke in the night.

Once Shoko got to sleep, she slept well (of course, waking for the loo at intervals, when she needed guidance to get there and back). But getting her settled to bed each night was still a challenge. She had always taken her time to get to bed, and resisted any attempt to hurry her (we had both been late birds, all through our marriage). But now it was qualitatively different. She would go upstairs, but not necessarily plan to go to bed. Instead, she pottered in the bedroom, checking her cupboards and drawers for a while. Then she began a circuit – to the loo, then the bathroom, then back to her toilet bag, with face cream in different tubes and jars. This circuit could be repeated several times, up to an hour, perhaps indefinitely. I needed to judge the right time to guide her to the next step, actually getting into bed. Once there, she would take her medicine, we would pray together, talk a bit and then I would put one of her books into her hand.

'Read this,' I would encourage her.

Quite often she would read a few pages and her eyes would begin to close. It was time to put out the light.

There were four or five Japanese books that she kept by her bed. My favourite was *Kotaishi Denka*,[12] some speeches of the Crown Prince, with a charming picture at the front, which Shoko always enjoyed looking at. A few pages were sufficient, almost every time, to bring refreshing sleep. I was so grateful to him for writing those speeches.

We were able to continue this pattern for several months. Tim's help was invaluable and he also came to visit. I was amazed, and grateful, to have somebody that I could turn to for practical advice whenever I needed it. He was always available, at the end of the phone, to give advice or just to talk. His experience, both as a doctor and with his friends with Alzheimer's, made his advice all the more relevant.

My sister suggested that I also needed somebody local to talk to, with whom I could be very open and frank as to how I was feeling. I decided to ask our vicar, Robin Weekes, if he would be willing to give me time. He immediately agreed and we started to meet every three weeks for about an hour. These sessions became another source of strength. Robin and his wife, Ursula, were already close friends. They had lived in India for some years, so we had a lot in common. They had also gone

---

[12] *Kotaishi Denka* (Tokyo: Meiseisya Co Ltd, 2010).

through intense suffering themselves, which gave them great empathy and warmth.

Robin listened, without being shocked or disturbed when I expressed my difficulties, frustrations and sometimes doubts. He asked questions about my well-being, what I was eating, how I was sleeping and so on. He was very fond of Shoko and would always greet her warmly when they met in church.

Talking to Robin helped me to reflect on what was happening to us and how I was responding. From childhood I had learned from my parents about a God who loved each of us personally. At the same time He was the Almighty Creator who was in control of everything. I had followed their faith and personally experienced God's love, expressed above all in Jesus. The familiar opening of the Lord's Prayer summed it up – 'Our Father in heaven'.[13]

Those words express the two sides of God's character – a Father who is loving and dependable and who is also all-powerful. Whatever happens is under His control, even when we don't understand how.

That had given a very secure framework for my life. Shoko shared it with me. We had thought about it, discussed with people of different views, advised and supported others in difficult situations.

But now?

'Now it has come to you … and you are dismayed,' said Job's friends in the familiar Old Testament story (Job 4:5).

---

[13] Matthew 6:9.

I couldn't compare myself to Job and his extraordinary suffering. But I knew I was finding it very difficult and disturbing. How long would this go on? Why was I finding it so hard?

Robin listened patiently, with no hint of criticism, as he also referred me back to the truths of the Bible. Two things stood out from our conversations:

When we suffer, God is with us. We ask 'Why?', but we may never find the answer. Perhaps 'Who?' is a better question. Who is with us when we suffer? The Gospel says that we are not alone, because God is with us.[14] When Jesus came into our world it meant that God came right down to our level and suffered along with us.

We have hope, because our relationship with God continues beyond death. I told Robin how our daughter had found it very sad that her mother was not the same as she was before. 'Yes,' he replied. 'Shoko is not as she was, and not as she will be.' He was referring to the hope of new life beyond this life, because of our relationship with God, who is alive and gives us life. 'He is not God of the dead, but of the living' said Jesus in Mark 12:27. And He Himself rose from death to confirm that. Robin linked this to Jesus' other promise in John's Gospel (14:1-3), words that would become very significant later.

Another truth, that Robin and Ursula didn't talk about, but modelled practically, to both of us, was the support that we receive from being part of a community of love and friendship.

---

14 Matthew 1:23.

I held on to what I was receiving and kept struggling on.

Tim and Robin became two pillars of support. I was already getting very solid support from the third one – family. My sister and brother had understood from the beginning, as we had all watched our father, and our mother looking after him. They gave their unstinting encouragement and constant support, and Elspeth, living nearby, was a frequent visitor. So was Adela, Sarah's mother-in-law.

Sarah and Jonathan had also been there right from the beginning, with full support from Tom and Elsa. Now Sarah began coming once a month, from Barcelona. Jonathan, in Tokyo, was much further away, but in 2017 he was able to make four visits, partly through his work.

Their visits were a vital encouragement to both of us. We sat together or they accompanied us on our regular visits to the supermarket or physiotherapy or church. They helped with cooking and tidying. They checked what Shoko was wearing and what I was wearing. They sang or played games with Shoko. They met Yuna, as well as other friends who were helping us. When the grandchildren came, we had a lot of fun. Shoko loved to play with them and sing together and they were all very sweet with her.

But it wasn't always easy for Sarah and Jonathan to visit, as they saw their mother changing each time. As the year went by, they might have wondered, as they arrived from their busy schedules and their own families, if they would be recognised. And after two or three days they would have to say goodbye again. On one occasion Sasha had come with Sarah and we went together to a family gathering. But Shoko was tired and didn't want to get out of the car. We tried to persuade her but didn't succeed. It was a difficult moment for us all and Sasha burst into tears. It was hard for her to see her beloved 'Baba' so different.

Sarah and Jonathan were completely supportive of me and what I was trying to do. Their perspective was slightly different, as they were not living with Shoko all the time. So they saw some things that I was missing – and occasionally missed things that I saw. It was always valuable to have their perspective, especially as they watched our interactions and my reactions, and gave me candid feedback and advice.

We had long conversations, discussing the current challenges or thinking about options and contingency plans for the future. How was I coping? What would they do if I got ill? We visited some care homes together. (Tim had wisely advised us to get detailed information about all the options – residential care, live-in care, respite care – so that we would be able to make the right choices at any time when we might need to.) We continued our conversations with regular emails and phone calls between the visits. I relied on their support and being able to keep in touch.

When Shoko spoke on the phone to them it was always: 'When are you coming?' She loved to see them and missed them when they left. She did forget, but I was surprised at how long she remembered and how deeply she felt. I wrote to Sarah:

6th March 2017

Dear Sarah,

We got back from the airport [where we dropped you with Tom and Sasha] and sat down for tea. Ma began crying, and said in Japanese, 'My tears are flowing.' At first she said it was because she couldn't feed any of you something nice (like ice cream, I suppose), but then she just said, 'I miss them so much.' We comforted each other with the thought that God is looking after you all, that Jonathan is coming next week and that you are coming again soon. She was really missing you and mentioned it again as we prepared to go out.

10
What Was So Difficult?

In July 2017 I wrote on behalf of us both to our friends:

Shoko really enjoys church, is happy to meet and greet people, and loves to make friends with children and babies. She plays the piano most days and loves to sing – hymns and Japanese songs. She is on the whole in good spirits, and always very loving and caring, but some days confused and anxious, which is hard for her.

Overall it has been demanding, and sometimes discouraging ...

So what was the difficulty?

In summary, Shoko was often confused about many things and this led to erratic and unpredictable behaviour. That in turn led to frustration for me and sometimes for her.

In the morning she had no difficulty dressing herself, but she wasn't always sure what she should put on. She might easily put on a blouse (or two) over her cardigan, or slippers without her socks. Taking them off could be difficult. I have always had cold hands and she found that very unpleasant. 'Your hands are so cold!' she would complain.

Leaving the house was a challenge. When I suggested that we go out, the immediate response was, 'I need to go to *oteārai*.' Off she would go. Meanwhile I needed to get her things ready in order – shoes, handbag, coat, gloves, scarf (depending on the season). These needed to be in place and available, as any break in sequence meant she would need to go to *oteārai* once more and we would have to start all over, or she might just say, 'I'm not going out.' Sometimes she wanted to put on some hand cream before going out and that would mean a side trip to the dining room, and then starting the circuit again, unless I had put the cream out in the hall for her. I also needed to get ready water, oranges, biscuits and so on to take with us.

Remember, we could not have all these things conveniently located in the hall, as Shoko would be worried about them being taken and would want to put them away. They had to be stored in suitable places, some of them upstairs. So it was a challenge to remember each item and bring them all together at the right time.

Things could be difficult to find if Shoko had put them away in a different place. I found it helpful to have two sets of things like gloves, scarves and reading glasses. I would keep a spare set in one of my drawers where Shoko wouldn't move them. There was a period when she constantly moved things or hid them to keep them safe. It was occasionally amusing to find a pair of slippers beautifully wrapped up and stored tidily in the fridge. But usually it was just irritating and sad. We couldn't find things when we needed them and Shoko would not be able to remember where they had been put. So we had to look for them. If I then suggested keeping them in a more convenient place, this could lead to an argument. We continued to have arguments about the china cupboard key.

When we had finally managed to leave the house and get into the car, the first task was fixing her seatbelt. This could be awkward as she would be holding her handbag and I needed to get the belt underneath it. And there were always those cold hands touching her – so unpleasant.

Getting to the table for meals was another logistical challenge. I would try to have everything hot and ready to serve, as she would have done in the past. She had always loved to eat things hot, especially *ramen*, which must be eaten immediately. But these days Shoko might come to the table when called, but then decide she needed to go to *oteārai* once again (or twice). By the time she came back things might be cold, though she didn't seem to mind.

When I suggested to Shoko that she come downstairs, for example for a meal, it wasn't always easy for her to do that. She would need to go to *oteārai* first, and then check that everything was in its place. If the bedroom door was open, she could easily be distracted to go back there and start doing something else. She would also be worried by lights that needed to be turned off. In short, anything that interrupted the sequence could result in not doing what we planned to do.

When we came out of the kitchen, she always checked carefully that the mat by the door was straight. She wanted things to be tidy (unlike her lazy husband) and couldn't relax if the rug in the hall was not straight. If I put my shoes on in a hurry and didn't lace them up at once, she was quite rightly disturbed and wanted me to tie them up before doing anything else.

Toilet paper was another source of anxiety. We could not leave a full roll in the downstairs bathroom because she worried about it being taken and would hide it somewhere else. I needed to keep just enough there to use, but not more. Shoko also tended to tear off pieces of toilet paper and store them in her drawers, in her handbag and other places. She needed to be sure she always had enough.

I couldn't persuade her to go for walks, because of her back. So our daily visit to Tesco, our local supermarket, became our main exercise. The staff greeted us with a smile, each time, and were very kind. Shoko didn't always enjoy it, as her back hurt her. Twenty-five metres in, she would stop and hold her back. 'Let's finish quickly,' she would say.

As we walked down the first aisle, she always wanted to buy some kitchen roll. I learned to accept things that she picked up, and then put them back on the shelf a bit later. Usually she didn't notice. By the time we got to the checkout she was anxious and impatient to leave. Often she was keen to visit *oteārai* at the store and I would hope that the disabled toilet was free, so I could accompany her. Otherwise she would disappear into the ladies' and I might wait a long time for her to emerge, or have to ask somebody else to check if she was all right.

A big challenge was how to occupy Shoko through the day in ways that would be enjoyable and stimulating. Previously we used to watch Japanese DVDs and had our favourite comedy series – *Tora-san*. We had seen the whole series except the last one. We had just bought it when Shoko said one evening, 'I don't like this. Horrible people.' We stopped watching TV. (Looking back, I wondered if she thought the people on the screen were really in our room. I had heard that other people with Alzheimer's couldn't distinguish TV characters from real people.)

She had always loved books but now she only read for a few minutes in bed. Nothing during the day. People recommended drawing or colouring, but she wasn't interested in that. Cooking and sewing were now beyond her reach. She wasn't interested in gardening, and going for walks had become problematic.

We played card games sometimes. But our main pleasure came from singing together. We had more than one hymn book but we settled on one from the 1960s. These were songs we had both known and loved for a long time. There were 100 songs, of which we knew eighty and definitely liked about sixty-five. Sometimes we would sing through the whole sixty-five, just the first verse of each. It would take us about an hour.

We also sang Japanese folk and children's songs. We were given some CDs with a good range and I was astonished at how many Shoko knew and could sing. She was able to teach me some, with the help of the song book, which I read slowly and laboriously. She would also play the piano, mostly with Yuna but occasionally with others.

She had six to eight hymns that she played, from memory or from the book. I was never quite sure which, as she would open the book to the right page but would sometimes be playing a different hymn, one of her favourites.

I was always amazed at the power of music and song to remain in the memory.[15] We had heard about this from others and it proved remarkably true. I made a playlist for her but she didn't listen to it very much. She preferred actually singing together.[16]

When Shoko's younger sister, Kazuko, visited from Japan with her husband, Haruo, Shoko knew who she was. But they sat opposite each other, not quite sure what to say. Then Haruo began a Japanese song and Shoko immediately picked it up: she knew the words and the tune. They sang several together and then Shoko went to the piano and played a hymn.

Their visit was a huge encouragement, though not easy for them to see Shoko so changed. What stayed in their minds and gave them joy was the music.

'I have never forgotten we sang a song with her, and we listened to a hymn that she played,' wrote Kazuko

---

[15] See especially Magnusson, *Where Memories Go*. Also www.playlistforlife.org.uk/music-and-dementia (accessed 3rd October 2019). Lee-Fay Low, *Live and Laugh With Dementia* (Chatswood, NSW: Exisle Publishing, 2014) has a useful chapter (chapter 10) with practical advice on how to apply this.

[16] Lee-Fay Low comments that singing may actually give more stimulus than listening, though that is valuable as well.

afterwards. 'She did not give expression to her thought well, but I felt her tenderness for me.'

Singing was great for perhaps an hour or so. But what about the rest of the time? I racked my brains and often felt guilty that I wasn't spending more time doing things that would occupy us together.

It reminded me of the time when our children were small and as parents we needed to find things to occupy them constructively and peacefully through the day. Sometimes that was easy, but sometimes it was difficult and tiring, for both parents and children. Time could drag and tired parents might wonder how they would get through the day. The difference was that with our children we could see their progress, almost daily. The direction was upwards. But in this case the direction was the opposite.

A book that I read later pointed out the similarities between children at different stages and the different stages of dementia. As I read it I could see (looking back) how Shoko had moved from the eight to twelve years old stage, when she could still travel somewhat independently, through five to seven, to her current stage of three to five, able to dress and care for herself, but needing much prompting and guidance.[17]

I had already noticed this similarity, even before reading the book. And I had realised the difference as well. Shoko was not a child but an adult with many years of experience and wisdom. She had been queen of her

---

[17] Lee-Fay Low, *Live and Laugh With Dementia*. It became important for me for its emphasis on the value of activities to go on engaging and occupying the person with Alzheimer's.

kitchen (and in fact of her whole household). I needed to respect that, while also recognising her limitations.

In summary, none of these things in themselves were serious problems. But taken together they could be very frustrating, especially with our different personalities. I was casual, while Shoko was often worried. I was impatient when things didn't go according to plan, while she was not troubled. I was on call from the time we got up until the time she was asleep. And I could never be sure when that would be: each evening there was the chance that she might not settle to sleep.

The pressure was relentless. It wasn't Shoko's fault and I wasn't against her. But it was hard not to be impatient, easy to speak cross words, difficult to be waiting: to go out, to sit at the table, to get to bed. How long?

I wrote to Sarah and Jonathan:

> *Some days are harder than others, as you know. On a hard day, it can be difficult to think of keeping going, while on a good day (like today so far) you wonder what the problem is.*

I was full of fear. Fear about getting through the days. Fear about how to settle her at night. From afternoon onwards that occupied my thoughts. I was often tense and worried.

I remembered some of my favourite words:

> There is no fear in love ... perfect love casts out fear.
> *1 John 4:18*

They were great for facing difficult situations or people. But what did they mean for me now?

Perhaps I needed to think more about Shoko, less about myself. She was not causing any of the problems. It was the horrible disease. If I focused on loving her and thinking how best to care for her, it made a difference.

Sometimes I would see people without obvious disabilities in the street and feel envious. But then I would realise, 'I have no idea what their situation is really like. What challenges might they be facing? Do they have hope, as we do?'

Then I would see an obviously disabled person, and realise that others might be facing difficulties too.

As we grappled with our situation, I found myself asking, 'Is this the same person? What has happened to my wife?'

11

Is This the Same Person?

Shoko had become very different.

When we went to the Cognitive Stimulation Therapy class, one of the others said ruefully, 'We are managing OK. But I just want my husband to be like he was before.'

That was what I wanted, and so did Sarah. 'I feel sad that my mother isn't as she used to be,' she said. We both knew it wouldn't happen.

The change had been quite gradual before, but now it was marked. Earlier we had seen changes but she had been very much the same person. Now she wasn't. What was happening to her?

Around this time our good friend Clare lent us a book: *I'm Still Here* by John Zeisel.[18] Reading it was a revelation.

Zeisel's basic point was that the person with Alzheimer's *is still a person with whom we can relate*, though it is a different relationship. It's the same person, but it's not the same person. We need to understand this change:

---

[18] John Zeisel, *I'm Still Here* (London: Piatkus, 2011).

we can't go back to the old relationship. *But we can build a new relationship.*

Alzheimer's is a terminal illness, Zeisel explained, but we can treat it, not necessarily with medicine, but by the way in which we relate and help to improve the quality of a person's life. For example, he listed the four As of Alzheimer's, which can be so disturbing when we encounter them: Agitation, Aggression, Anxiety and Apathy.[19] But these are not caused directly by Alzheimer's. They are 'side effects', responses to the effects of the disease on a person.

I read his list and checked it against our experience.

Agitation: this comes from the lack of ability to initiate for oneself. As a result the person can become restless or tend to perform repeated actions. Was Shoko's constant return to *oteārai* an example of this?

Aggression: the person is no longer able to control their impulses and so they act in a way that they would not normally have done. They might strike out in order to express their frustration or pain at what is being done to them. Shoko was never aggressive in her behaviour, in the way I later read about. But sometimes when I tried to help her get dressed, or undressed, and she didn't like what I was doing, she would slap me, or tell me, 'Get away!' It was the only way to express her frustration.

Anxiety: the person no longer has a clear picture of time or of causal relationships. Why is this happening? What is happening next? Anybody would become anxious in those circumstances. Was this why Shoko became so

---

[19] Ibid, p 35.

worried that things were missing? What was the cause of that?

Apathy: when a person can no longer perceive or remember the future, they can't plan – something that all of us do unconsciously all the time. When that ability goes the person may retreat into apathy, not doing anything because there doesn't seem to be anything interesting to do. Shoko would occasionally act like this. But more often she would respond by becoming restless and wanting to go out. Or she would say, 'Let's eat something really nice, something sweet.'

Zeisel went on to show how we could *treat* these four As, beginning with the social environment, how we communicate, how we behave, what activities we take part in. Then there is the physical environment, the arrangement of the house and garden, or the places that we visit. Finally there can be medical and pharmacological interventions, for example to help a person sleep, as our GP had prescribed for Shoko, or in some cases to moderate their behaviour.[20]

The different parts of the brain are affected in different ways by Alzheimer's. Some, like the ability to plan or organise, go very quickly. Others remain, such as facial expressions, responses to touch, singing, ways of finding your way around. The person with Alzheimer's often finds it difficult to distinguish reality from illusions, perhaps what they see on television. They might have hallucinations or imagine somebody is there. But an important part of the brain connected with experiencing

---

[20] Ibid, pp 41-48.

emotions, known as the *amygdala* (because it is shaped like an almond), remains strong.[21] Shoko's ability to show affection and express her love was as strong as ever.

As Sarah, Jonathan and I read Zeisel's book, it made so much sense of what had been puzzling us. We began to understand what might have been going on in Shoko's mind.

Zeisel gave helpful rules of communication. The most challenging was, 'Don't say "Don't".' Instead we should 'distract' and 'redirect' or 'divert'.[22] The other person is on a fixed course and you can't change that. But distraction and diversion do work, just as they do with small children.

That was easy to understand, much harder to practise. 'Don't' was my default response. As a teacher I used to like an orderly classroom, with students sitting quietly. I loved to facilitate discussion (and I was good at doing that), but it should be organised and under control. Shoko had always been more impulsive. Now her responses and actions were much harder to predict. She didn't fit into what I was expecting. I had to learn how to distract her and find new ways of redirecting her impulses.

Reading the book gave us this challenge. We can *choose to build a new kind of relationship*, or we can choose not to.

There is both sadness and joy in this transition. We were experiencing the sadness. We remembered the 'strong woman' of Gunma, the 'adventurer' who had travelled the world, crossed several cultures and brought up her family with her love and strength. It was hard to

---

[21] Ibid, p 68.
[22] Ibid, p 148.

think that now she could barely leave the house. It was hard to let go of the characteristics we had treasured. But now we could enter into a new relationship. She was not the same, yet she *was* still the same: still loving, still hospitable, still smiling, despite the uncertainty and confusion that she must be experiencing each day.

Another book that we all read at this time was the brilliant and quirky *Contented Dementia* by Oliver James.[23] It was based on the experiences of Penny Garton with her mother. The main lesson seemed to be to protect the person with Alzheimer's from being bombarded with new information and to support them through the 'photographs' of their old memories.

Some professionals gave a cautious approval of the SPECAL approach pioneered by this book (Specialised Early Care for Alzheimer's).[24] Others were very critical. We found it gave us really helpful pointers.

For example, don't keep asking questions of the person you are relating to. Learn from them, rather than the other way round. Enter into their world. And always agree, never interrupting what they want to say or do.

That was challenging, and not all the suggestions worked for us. But we found the central theme extremely

---

[23] Oliver James, *Contented Dementia* (London: Vermilion, 2009).
[24] Atkins, *First Steps to Living with Dementia*, pp 57-59, is cautiously approving. The Alzheimer's Society is critical: www.alzheimers.org.uk/about-us/policy-and-influencing/what-we-think/specialised-early-care-alzheimers-special (accessed 3rd October 2019). William Cutting, *Dementia: A Positive Response* (Exeter: Onward and Upwards, 2018), pp 153-163, is positive.

valuable. In the end it was similar to what John Zeisel had been saying: respect the person, give them a sense of personal worth, a sense that they still have control over what they can do, that they can relate to others with some kind of confidence and optimism. They are still people.

We needed to be with them in their current experience, not trying to reason with them in a purely rational way but instead entering into their world, what they were feeling and thinking. We needed to start from their perspective. We also needed to build on their interests and experience of life, the things in which they were experts and which we could learn from them. We had to learn how to make connections with that past, so they could go on experiencing it in the present.

I could see that Yuna was very good at doing this as she talked with Shoko and drew her out. Shoko would tell her a lot about her past. Sometimes, if I came in and caught the tail end of the conversation, I realised it wasn't fully accurate. But that didn't matter.

Clare lent us another book, heavily annotated. *Where Memories Go* by Sally Magnusson.[25] It was a wonderful account of her family's experience with their mother as they coped with her dementia. We loved the detailed accounts of their actual situation and the many beautiful insights that rang so true to our experience. Sally Magnusson also reflected on the current systems for supporting people with dementia – and more often the lack of them. That matched our situation too.

---

25 Magnusson, *Where Memories Go*.

Reading these books began to widen our experience. We could see many common threads. But we could also see that everybody's experience was slightly different. Our brains and personalities are so marvellously complex that each person is affected in their own unique way.

Later we found other books, many published very recently, that gave further insights. We were still learning.

I reflected on Jesus' words, 'do not be anxious about tomorrow' (Matthew 6:34). Was He right? Was it possible not to think or worry about the future? I struggled with this. It was very difficult not to think ahead. 'All our lives we are trained to do that,' said my brother. On the other hand, each day was different and unpredictable. So I had to take each day as it came.

Could I learn to start each day: 'Thank you for this day; take us through it with joy'?

To finish each day: 'Thank you for bringing us through'?

John Zeisel's advice was very similar: live in the moment, like the person you are relating to.

12
'You're Not My Husband'

Shoko had times of confusion as far back as January 2016, when we went to Japan and she thought she was still in London. At the time we didn't realise what was going on in her mind: we knew that she wasn't settled, but didn't understand how confused she was.

Now her confusion was much more evident. One day we arrived home in the car and saw a lady from Home Instead waiting outside the house. She had brought a potential carer to meet us. I greeted them but Shoko didn't want to get out of the car. She didn't realise that we had reached home and she didn't want to meet anybody. I tried to persuade her but it didn't work. Then I remembered the advice from various sources: don't Disagree; instead Distract and Divert. So I quickly explained to our guests, got back into the car and we drove around the block. This time when we came back, she was happy enough to come in and serve tea to our guests. Distraction had worked!

The same thing began to happen more often, when we came back from shopping or other trips. She would be unwilling to get out.

'We haven't come home yet; we need to keep going.'

I didn't argue but would leave the shopping in the house, then get back into the car and drive around the block. It usually worked, but sometimes we needed to make two trips before she was settled.

There were other times when we came back into the house and she felt that we couldn't stay. We were in somebody else's house, or she thought there were people staying in our house and we needed to go. We must leave at once. Once we wrote them a note, which she dictated, and then left the house:

> *Thank you for the nice food.*
> *Sarah enjoyed being in your home.*
> *You are welcome any time.*

Sometimes the confusion arose because 'somebody' was telling her what she should do. These 'people' were sometimes a man and sometimes a woman. They might be upstairs or downstairs and quite often they were telling her things that were not nice for her to hear.

'Shhh, don't talk so loudly,' she would say to me. 'Those people... don't you know?'

'There are twelve people downstairs. We need to prepare food for them. Then we need to make their beds...'

Sometimes 'he'/'she'/'they' had come to her in her bedroom and said, 'Don't do that... You can't have these books...'

She would be worried and so happy to see me.

Sometimes 'they' told her not to take her pills. She quite often hesitated to take them, not wanting to take too many (rightly). But when the people spoke to her, they might tell her that the pills were very bad ('*dame*' in Japanese) and would kill her.

These incidents usually passed fairly quickly, but occasionally we would have an extended conversation about what 'he' had said and how she had responded. I would reassure her that she had done nothing wrong and had responded really well. She had nothing to worry about.

On one occasion we got into the car to go to Tesco. Shoko was worried about money: 'Fusako [her older sister in Japan] needs money… I should have given some to that man… I will write to ask his forgiveness.'

We finished our shopping and got back into the car.

'You're not leaving tonight, are you?' she asked me. 'How will Robin take us home if you are leaving? Can't you stay with us tonight? That would be wonderful.'

But when we came home she didn't want to go in: 'This is not our house.'

We went round the block and this time we went into the house.

'Shhh, that man is upstairs.'

We sat down and she was convinced that he was coming.

'No,' I said. 'He's not coming tonight.'

'Yes, he is.'

'I know he's not coming because he telephoned to tell me. He will contact us again tomorrow.'

'Are you sure?'

This carried on for nearly thirty minutes, going round and round, again and again. Finally we managed to drop it and began to sing one of our favourite songs about a Japanese doll.

A few days later, as we left the doctor's she turned to speak to the receptionist: 'It's not really his fault. He didn't mean it…'

The receptionist was puzzled but smiled kindly.

'Goodbye,' said Shoko. 'Thank you. You are very kind.'

Now the receptionist was touched and thanked Shoko in turn.

Another time, as we left the house, Shoko was concerned about Sarah (who was in Barcelona). 'We must leave a message for her.'

She sat down to write it:

> *My dear Sarah*
> *We are going tough [= out] yet but we are come*
> *home quite soon.*
> *With Shoko and Robin-san*
> *With love*
> *We'll be home soon.*

The message was clear though the words were confused.

Like many with Alzheimer's, Shoko also began to lose her sense of smell. That didn't particularly matter. But it affected her sense of taste. She mixed things up – sweet and savoury – which she would not have done before. And she lost interest in dishes she had previously enjoyed, particularly some Japanese ones. She had loved *umeboshi*, the sour pickled plum, and other Japanese pickles. Now they had no attraction and her choice of daily meals became quite simple and limited (we still enjoyed *sushi* from time to time!). This made things easier for my limited skills, but I felt sorry as she had been such a food lover.

Shoko also found it more difficult to see things (another common effect of Alzheimer's). She would sometimes not notice things that were right in front of her, or have difficulty identifying which door led to which room.

Despite this, she could still spot a mark on my shirt from right across the room, or notice that my shoes were undone, or my hair was untidy. In this respect nothing had changed from the day that we got married.

Now she had also developed a beady eye for anything that I had not put away. She would seize upon it like a magpie: either something nice to eat, like the tin of biscuits on the side table, or something that she felt needed to be put away, which I might then find difficult to trace. I learned to put everything away promptly (good for keeping the place tidy).

The most difficult confusion was when she didn't recognise me. This was rare. It only happened three times in all, when she was going to bed. The first time, she wasn't very happy because she thought I was pressing her to go to bed. So she said to me crossly, 'I'll tell my husband as soon as he comes back.'

Surprised, I replied that I was her husband.

'You're not my husband,' she said, scornfully. I was dismayed and tried to persuade her that I really was.

'I'm Robin, your husband. Look at me... look at my clothes... of course I'm your husband.'

She wasn't convinced.

I didn't know what to do. It was the moment I had been dreading. 'So it has come to this,' I thought. 'The moment that all the books and stories tell you is inevitable. She doesn't know me any more.'

As I stood there, thinking what I could say next to convince her, I remembered the advice: don't Disagree; instead Distract and Divert. So I went downstairs, opened the front door and rang the bell. I came in, shut the door loudly and said, 'Hello, here I am.'

It worked.

'Where have you been?' she said. 'I was looking for you.'

All was well.

It happened twice more, in the next two weeks. These times it didn't work quite so smoothly. Shoko accepted me but was still puzzled and wondered where her husband was. However, after a few minutes she settled down again.

These incidents happened only three times and after that Shoko didn't deny that I was her husband, in the same way. But later she began to talk about *Otōsan* as a third person. *Otōsan* ('Papa') was what she called me all the time these days. But now, quite often, she would say to me 'How is *Otōsan*?' or 'Where is *Otōsan*?'

As we were leaving the house she would say, 'We need to tell *Otōsan*, we need to leave a note for him.' In the evening she would often say, 'I wonder when *Otōsan* is coming back. Where is he?'

I didn't try to argue or say that I was *Otōsan*. I simply said, 'He's gone out for his work,' and she was satisfied with that. Sometimes I would say, 'He will come back in the morning.'

Was *Otōsan* a combination, perhaps, of her own father, in some shadowy sense, and me? Somehow he became this third person, who was often with us. She liked him and thought he was great. He was kind and understanding. He was much better than me, especially when I was trying to help her to bed. I found myself quite jealous, thinking about him. But we managed to get on quite well with him, as he didn't intrude and she only thought of him from time to time. And even when she was speaking about him, she was still always warm and kind towards me and told me she loved me.

Well – not quite always. She did also get very cross, if I was pressing her to do something – to get ready for bed, take her medicine, go out or change her blouse.

'*Otōsan*' – referring to *me* this time, not that third party – 'is a very strange person,' she would say in disgust. 'I don't like you. You are rough.'

I couldn't fully work out who she thought I was. But it didn't matter, if she loved me.

13

An Increasing Sense of Loss

Dementia is a condition whose signature symptoms are those of loss.[26]

For Sarah and Jonathan, it was hard. They missed the letters that Shoko used to write. And when they visited, their mother wasn't the same.

The last letter she wrote to Sarah was in 2016. 'I heard Mummy's voice again,' Sarah said, when she read it.

But that was the last one, and by the following year even phone conversations became more and more limited. Sometimes Shoko was quite engaged and happy to talk, though not for very long. At other times she didn't want to take the phone. She might say 'Give them my love' or just not say anything. They accepted that but it was another loss.

When they came to visit, Shoko's face lit up and she would become very jolly and playful. After supper, as she

---

[26] Atkins, *First Steps to Living with Dementia*, p 84.

left for bed, she would tell them, 'Help yourselves and eat as much as you like. Make yourselves at home.'

She would make funny faces, blow them kisses and go upstairs. But the next day she would come downstairs, look into the dining room and see one of them there.

'Shhh… who is that?' she would ask me.

They learned to respond by introducing themselves again. And as she spoke to them, she would relax and recognise them once more, though she might ask, 'How are your parents? Is your mother well?'

I was with her all the time, which was both easier and harder. I could be with her in all her moods, good and not so good. I could experience her love all the time and I didn't have to say goodbye. At one level our communication was very deep, deeper than ever. But it was quite narrow. We couldn't talk about what we had done that day, or what we were planning to do. Conversation about anything in the present moment was strictly limited:

'Now we're going to go out… It's time for us to eat… Look at those beautiful roses in the garden…' (Shoko still loved beautiful flowers.)

We could talk about the past and look at our pictures. But the people in the photo albums became less and less familiar. Earlier, when she saw our engagement picture, she knew it was us. But as time went on that changed. She was excited to see *Otōsan* in the picture and could identify him with me. But she also asked, 'I wonder what happened to him?' Or on another occasion – 'Is that his wife in the picture?' – it was more difficult to realise that the girl in the picture was her. Sometimes she did get it, but more often she didn't.

I wrote in my journal:

15th May 2017

Last night we were looking at our engagement and wedding pictures in the album. You were able to connect with them – which wasn't always the case.

'Who is that person in white?' you asked. 'Oh, it's me,' you said. 'And that is you… We are holding hands… Can we stay together always?'

You were so beautiful. My eyes devoured the pictures. And I thought, you are still beautiful and I love you more than ever. Your face, your skin, your whole personality, your loving spirit to everybody you meet, friend or stranger.

As you lay down later, ready to sleep, you smiled at me and spoke loving words, looking just like your wedding picture.

I wish I could go back and live it all again with you. I know you so much better now. I might make fewer mistakes.

Shoko was finding sentences difficult to finish, or she couldn't find the words she wanted. She spoke mostly in Japanese, but also in English. When it was Japanese, I couldn't always follow, because my vocabulary was limited and she couldn't translate for me, or repeat what she had just said. At other times what she said didn't really make much sense. The same was true in English; conversations could wander, sometimes with a clear underlying theme, but not always.

For example, in the car:

'Have you got that [*something*]…? They are coming just now… We forgot to bring… [*can't get the words out*]… you know, North Cheam… [*the destination on the bus approaching us*]… I wanted to buy it but it was so expensive, but the other day it was so cheap…'

At home: 'They are telling me to go. Tomorrow a man comes, it's the village where the wind blows, or maybe the moisturising cream…'

What was she saying? Then I realised she was reading the titles of the books on her table and the label on the jar of her cream in front of her.

One night when she didn't settle, she came downstairs and was clearly a bit worried about something. She took a piece of paper and wrote, 'I don't like Billy Graham.'

This famous preacher had been one of her favourite people. She had met him in Japan. But as she saw the song book lying there with his name on the cover, he became the focus of her concern.

June Andrews quotes a person remembering her grandmother talking, 'chattering away, with mixed up words … and then a clear phrase would come through, out of context, like a clearing in fog'.[27]

Wendy Mitchell describes her experience of the fog on bad days, when she would be 'floating in and out of consciousness … A good day can turn foggy at the turn of a page.'[28]

That must have been what Shoko felt.

---

[27] June Andrews, *Dementia: The One-Stop Guide* (London: Profile Books, 2015), p 89.

[28] Mitchell, *Somebody I Used to Know*, pp 131, 294.

Our wedding day in Madras, 4th January 1969

Shoko in Paris, 2006

Shoko at home, 2017

These times of loss meant frequent tears. Sometimes tears for what we were losing; sometimes tears of joy, as I thought of Shoko's love. Sometimes tears thinking of other people's love and kindness.

Through all the times of loss there were many good times as well. For example:

Sunday morning in church. This was a highlight of the week. Shoko never tired of going there. At first she would be struggling to find her glasses, looking through her handbag, trying to open the hymn book or the Bible, not quite sure which was the right book for the time. She would stand to sing or sometimes stay seated, with a book open but not always singing the words. As the months passed, she didn't need her glasses because she didn't try to open the book any more. Sometimes she seemed sleepy, especially through the sermon. But she was always happy to be there and at the end we would sit together listening to the music, watching the children go past, not in any hurry to move. And then she would greet our friends with a smile, whether she knew who they were or not. She was very fond of our vicar. 'I like that man,' she said, when she saw him in the pulpit.

People were always kind and friendly, greeting both of us with affection and warmth, talking to her. It was an oasis for me as well: joining in the singing and the prayers; listening to the Bible being taught, with amazing relevance; being reassured by the affection and concern of friends who understood something of our situation and who we knew were praying for us.

Watching Shoko's love of children. One of the joys of church was meeting small children. Shoko loved to watch them, talk to them and sometimes touch small babies. We also saw them at the supermarket. Shoko might be complaining about her back, finding it tiring to walk. But if she saw a child she would smile and relax. Sometimes she sang to them in Japanese, a favourite song about doves. They would be fascinated and the parents loved it as well.

Welcoming people at home. It was always good to have friends visiting. Sometimes Shoko was not engaged and would sit quietly, even vacantly. At other times she enjoyed talking to them, listening to them. Somehow she could tell that these were people she knew and loved.

Whoever it was, she was always concerned for them and wanted to offer them tea and something to eat. Our good friends Richard and Brenda came to visit. Brenda and Shoko had been roommates at London Bible College and had remained close friends for many years. But Shoko's focus that day was on Richard sitting opposite. She wanted him to eat. I brought out a cake and cut a slice for everybody.

'Give him some more,' she said. 'Give him some more.'

I gave Richard a second slice and suggested to him that he accept it. He was happy to do so and told us that he loved cake. Soon after that Shoko wanted to cut him another slice.

'I think he has had enough,' I said, but she insisted.

'Don't be mean!'

She went to him with another piece, and embraced him warmly. Richard seemed happy to have the cake.

'Give him some more,' she said.

So we put some more cake in a box for them to take. Shoko was satisfied.

Others might not get so much cake but they enjoyed singing together. We would open the songbook and start singing from it. Sometimes Shoko would play the piano for them. Singing was always a pleasure for her.

She loved Yuna whenever she came, but never, ever, remembered her name or talked about her when she was not there.

I wrote in my journal:

24th June 2017

Today I read this beautiful poem celebrating a wonderful wife:

'She is far more precious than jewels ...

The heart of her husband trusts in her ...

Her children rise up and call her blessed ...'
(Proverbs 31:10-31)

It's an A-Z (literally, in Hebrew) of all her qualities and accomplishments. I cried as I read it: so true of Shoko

- *she looked after her family with such energy and hard work*

- *she was bold and enterprising, wise with money and made good plans for investing it and developing our house*

- *she cared for others with great generosity, whatever their background.*

'Enjoy life with the wife whom you love, all the days of your ... life that he has given you.' (Ecclesiastes 9:9)

I did enjoy her. But sometimes I felt lonely because our communication was now so limited.

14
Invitation to Love?

'I try to picture your life, without much success,' wrote a thoughtful friend. 'Unpredictable; focused on another's needs; foreclosing long-term plans; allowing each day, week, month to open up as it will … Personal plans – to write, to go somewhere, to pray?? – are shelved.'

Another friend wrote:

> *Dear Robin, you all seem to be doing so well, but you do convey just how tiring it is to manage the swings between the joys and sorrows as well as the physical struggles together.*

I wrote back:

> *Thank you for your warm and encouraging words. You picked up 'tiredness' and I think that is my overriding feeling much of the time – both the day-to-day challenges and the long-term.*

I was certainly tired. For caregivers, there is unremitting pressure. They sometimes feel as if they can't go on. It's lonely and exhausting.[29]

Around this time I read two helpful books.

Robertson McQuilkin's wife was diagnosed with Alzheimer's at the age of fifty-five and lived to be eighty.[30] So he cared for her for twenty-five years, during twelve of which she was in a wheelchair and unable to speak. His love and devotion for her were remarkable. His book was moving, but I found it challenging, as he never seemed to complain. When I read the book a second time, I could discern some of the struggles that he also faced and that was encouraging to me.

Finding Grace in the Face of Dementia was written by John Dunlop,[31] a geriatric physician who also cared for both his own parents with Alzheimer's. So he wrote with medical authority but also very practically. His book was accurate, compassionate and honest. He understood, from both the outside and the inside.

John Dunlop had a whole chapter on the challenges for the primary caregiver. As I read it I ticked off each one. The demands were physical, mental, social, emotional and spiritual. I realised that he understood our situation.

But then how should I respond in order to keep going? He made it clear that the caregivers' role is a calling to serve and to love. There are different ways to express this,

---

[29] See Magnusson, *Where Memories Go*, pp 286-288.
[30] Robertson McQuilkin, *A Promise Kept* (Carol Stream, IL: Tyndale House Publishers, 1998).
[31] John Dunlop, *Finding Grace in the Face of Dementia* (Wheaton, IL: Crossway, 2017).

depending on the situation, whether the loved one continues at home or not, and other factors.

Another friend wrote, around the same time:

> *It amazes me how the Lord invites us to love more and more deeply in ways we would not have thought of when we were younger ... Well done. You and Shoko are in my prayers.*

I didn't really want to accept this 'invitation'. It was too challenging. But ultimately it was also moving and encouraging. It was a calling and there was a purpose. Perhaps I would find out more about what that purpose might be as time went on.

Friends and books also pointed out the need for caregivers to look after their own needs and to find practical, hands-on help from others.

'You need a break,' said my GP friend, Tim. 'Allow yourself to be selfish; don't neglect yourself.'

> If you fail to meet your basic needs, you will very quickly burn out and the quality of your care will deteriorate ... Recognise right from the beginning that providing care for someone with dementia is not a one-person job.[32]

This was the same advice I had received earlier. In response I had worked at building up a support team – family, friends, church members, carers, professional help. With their support we could continue. Without it we would have been lost.

---

[32] Atkins, *First Steps to Living with Dementia*, p 90.

That help was important for both of us. Shoko enjoyed and benefited from those who came to visit, from her weekly time in church, from the regular outings to our physio. Though she was so dependent on me, she needed all the others as well.

June Andrews emphasises the importance of friends to support both the caregiver and the person living with Alzheimer's.[33] Without them they are in danger of social isolation. We *need* friends, she says. They can give practical help across a range of areas, from food to financial matters, health issues, going for a walk, and more. One of our friends turned up from time to time, bringing a complete meal which he left with us.

Above all, friends give the gift of their time by keeping in touch, whether through visits or phone calls, letters or emails. We were experiencing this, as friends contacted us and as we worked at keeping them informed. There was a small group whom I could contact any time, by phone or email, to tell them about particular needs. They were committed to supporting us, by praying and by their practical help.

When friends came to visit, Shoko's apparent response varied. Sometimes she might not appear interested, while at other times she engaged warmly, especially if there was cake to offer. (And she would always respond to a song.) Some might have wondered if it was worth it. But each visit was important to her – 'Come again,' she would say – even if she forgot soon afterwards. She had great pleasure while they were there. And every visit was an

---

[33] June Andrews, *Dementia: The One-Stop Guide*, pp 75-98.

encouragement to me, to meet old friends, to share our experience with them, to know that they were thinking of us, to feel their love and concern.

In my journal I wrote:

3rd July 2017

Pure, unmediated love.

When inhibitions are reduced and there are few distractions our relationship becomes direct. There are no barriers.

You express it in your words to me, or sometimes to others about me; in acts of caring all the time. When I come home you stretch out your arms: 'Otōsan, I love you so much.' Then you want to feed me: 'Dozo... tabete kudasai... what would you like? Have this cake...'

It's very powerful, almost painful.

When you are lying down, ready to sleep, sometimes you touch my cheek with your warm hands and whisper words of love. Tonight you said, 'I love you and I am so happy to be with you. It's good to remember, as we go to bed. Thank you, Lord, for giving such a good person to me.'

Set me as a seal upon your heart,
as a seal upon your arm;
for love is strong as death ...
Its flashes are flashes of fire,
a most vehement flame.
Many waters cannot quench love,
neither can floods drown it.
Song of Solomon 8:6-7 (RSV)

15
Ready for the Long Haul?

It had taken three months, over the summer of 2017, to find the team of carers and get them settled in. We had got into a kind of routine, with carers, or friends, coming most afternoons from Monday to Friday. We were so grateful for their help. At first Shoko was a little puzzled by these people coming and sometimes seemed happy when they left. But as time went on, she got to know them better and would smile when they came into the room. As soon as they left, she forgot that they had come, but she enjoyed their company while they were there.

In July 2017 I tried something new. I asked Yuna to come one evening to give Shoko her supper, help her to bed and stay overnight. That meant that I could spend a night away and get a small break. The first time I went to stay nearby with one of the church caretakers. It was difficult to relax. I was waiting for Yuna's text messages, which came throughout the evening. She was actually fine and having a good time with Shoko. They ate supper together and Yuna helped her to bed, seemingly without difficulty. I finally slept and woke up early to receive Yuna's messages in the morning. The whole thing went well, and I was so relieved. It wasn't much of a break, as I didn't relax at all, but I was happy that Shoko had been well-settled and that this experiment was working.

The next time I was able to relax much more. I went to my sister's house for the evening. It was quite strange to be out of the house and sitting at table with others, without Shoko there. I had not been anywhere without her for several months. It was difficult to engage in 'normal' conversation with 'normal' people. I sat silently throughout the meal. Fortunately, that was not a problem, as Elspeth and her husband, James, were both well-able to sustain any conversation!

We continued the pattern every two or three weeks, and those nights out were a great help. I could sleep through the night and into the morning, knowing that Shoko was actually having a good time with Yuna. She would greet me happily when I returned, without a sense of having missed me.

However, around August I found that Shoko was not settling to sleep at all. She would get into bed and then get up and want to go downstairs and potter around, with no inclination to go back to bed.

I found the evenings and nights stressful, as I could never be sure whether Shoko would settle to sleep or not. In one sense it didn't matter, but in another sense it did. If I couldn't sleep, I knew I would become tired out and unable to look after her properly. We would both be up at least three times a night (on a few bad nights, five or six times) to help her go to the loo. Usually we went to sleep quickly afterwards and it was not a problem. But if she were not going to settle, or would be up for extended times, that would be different and I knew I wouldn't be able to manage.

Three things helped our situation. I consulted my friend Tim, and Phil Parker, the community dementia nurse. They both reminded me how important it was to have a calm, winding-down evening pattern. I was getting frustrated and stressed when Shoko didn't settle, or got up. I would speak crossly to her, and it had no effect, or might make her cross in return.

I realised that I needed to change my attitude and stay calm, whatever happened.

Secondly, I decided to stop our current practice of Shoko playing the piano after supper. I had encouraged this, as it seemed so good for her. But I wondered if it was too stimulating for her: often she didn't want to stop playing.

I wrote to Tim:

> *The last few days have been a lot better at night. Shoko has been moving much more smoothly towards bed and then getting to sleep quite quickly...*
>
> *As I mentioned before, the first key has been my attitude: I have really been helped to stay calm and patient. But also the change from playing the piano after supper does seem to have made a difference. It began by accident, as one night she didn't feel like playing and we looked at a book instead, and I realised how that helped her to become relaxed and drowsy. Playing the piano was relaxing but it was also waking her up at a time, after supper, when she was beginning to feel sleepy. Now I encourage her to*

play earlier in the evening, and she also plays when
Yuna is here. So she is still getting that stimulus.

Thirdly, in consultation with Tim and Phil (and our GP), it was agreed that we should increase the sleeping tablets. She was taking half-strength and so we increased it to the normal dose for adults.

As a result of this combination, Shoko was able to settle to sleep much more easily and deeply. There were no side effects, but she dozed sometimes in the day and generally that made her feel more relaxed. This new pattern carried on quite effectively for several months. She settled well in nine out of ten nights. I thought I could handle the one night in ten.

'4th October 2017. This is going to be a long haul,' I wrote in my journal. I was reflecting on the fact that our situation might go on for a long time.

At the beginning of that year, when Shoko declined so suddenly, I assumed she might not last beyond the summer. A very good friend with Alzheimer's had declined sharply and died within months, just two years earlier. But now Shoko was in good health physically and in good spirits as well. The day before, when Adela came, they were laughing and joking, teasing each other. Just before that, Shoko had spoken to Sarah on her birthday.

'You are my dear Mummy,' said Sarah.

'And you are my lovely daughter,' Shoko replied.

There was a real connection between them.

Shoko was managing day-by-day with help from Yuna and the others. Her sleep was good and the new carers seemed to have settled in. I was able to go out for four hours a day most days. We were in a settled routine again.

I decided to return to my earlier writing projects, which had been on hold.

In an article that I saw at this time a husband described how he watched and checked, helped and lovingly explained things to his wife who had Alzheimer's.[34] I was happy to try to continue doing the same.

'You are more at peace,' my sister wrote to me. It was true.

But at the same time, it was a challenge. 'How do I respond?' I wrote in my journal. I needed perseverance and wisdom for each day.

How long would it continue? It was impossible to say. I didn't think it would be twenty-five years like Robertson McQuilkin, but there was no way of knowing. When I asked Phil, he told me that the prognosis for Alzheimer's ranged from two to twenty years. He knew that wasn't very helpful and added that the most common was between seven and nine years. But everybody emphasised again and again that you could never tell. Each person was different.

I was up and down, emotionally and physically.

I still found the evenings and nights stressful. The slightly stronger medication was a great help, but it didn't always work the same way. Each day was different, as my 2017 journal showed:

---

[34] *The Guide*, magazine of the Raynes Park and West Barnes Residents' Association, September 2017. Author and article title unknown.

Sunday, 8th October

A difficult day. Shoko was tired because she got up early and was unsettled all afternoon. But after 4.00 we sang a bit, listened to hymns on the internet and she played the piano. My challenge: how do I continue to occupy her each day? What good activities can I introduce for her?

Monday, 9th October

Shoko had a good sleep and was so much more relaxed all day. In the afternoon I worked in the garden and she occupied herself. Then we had tea together. Her personality has become very sweet and gracious to me.

Tuesday, 10th October

What a difference a bad night makes! I felt quite discouraged in the morning and was cross with Shoko because she resisted me while I helped her to get dressed. 'Stop it,' I shouted, and she burst into tears. I felt so bad. It wasn't her fault. I said sorry at once. Shoko was quiet for a while but she forgot and didn't hold it against me. That afternoon I had a good talk with Robin Weekes (our vicar).

Wednesday 11th October

What a difference a good night makes! We both slept well.

Spiritually, too, I was up and down.

I was praying, holding on to what I believed and experiencing God's love and care, especially through family and friends. At the same time I was discouraged, complaining and wondering how long I could continue, feeling sad to see Shoko's condition. It wasn't that I was saying, 'Why me?' That question didn't fit. But it was definitely 'Poor me', again and again.

I was encouraged by an email from a friend in Sri Lanka: when he was facing difficulties he turned to the Psalms, where he found this amazing combination of trusting and thanking God, while at the same time groaning and complaining directly to God – 'lamenting'. That was exactly my experience. Lament and faith together. But I often felt guilty about it.

The pressure continued.

16
Two Prayers That Made a Difference

Right back at the beginning of 2017, when things had suddenly become difficult, I had read about a woman who was going through very difficult times in her life. Her husband had some big problems. So she was praying for the Lord to change him. But as she did so she felt that God was saying that *she* needed to change. She needed to pray that the Lord would changer *her*.[35]

It hit me like a thunderbolt. My situation was very different. But that was what *I* needed to pray: 'Lord, change *me*.' I was troubled by Shoko's condition, angry, impatient, upset. *I* needed to change. I was not angry with her. I was angry about her condition. But it affected all my attitudes. I was also very controlling, as Sarah had pointed out to me, more than once. I wanted her to do things in a certain way, for example at meals, or going out, or getting to bed. I found it difficult when she didn't, as was happening increasingly. And I recognised other areas

---

[35] Stormie Omartian, *Out of Darkness* (Eugene, OR: Harvest House Publishers, 2015).

in which my behaviour towards her had not been right, both now and in the past. I had not always valued her as I should. Suddenly I remembered attitudes and actions which had blocked our relationship at different times. I felt ashamed at the memories.

I realised how much I needed to repent and seek forgiveness, from Shoko and from God.

That week I had preached in church on Paul's attitude of contentment, which was not just about money but a deep attitude of accepting and trusting in God's wise and fatherly care, whatever the situation, through the strength that Christ gave him (Philippians 4:10-19).

I realised I was *not* contented.

As I prayed, I felt my attitude was changing. When I spoke to Shoko and tried to explain that I was sorry, she said, 'What you are saying is difficult to understand. Is there a problem?'

'No, there is no problem. It's just that I love you.'

Later, Sarah and Jonathan both expressed their surprise – and pleasure – at the way in which I was able to look after Shoko. They never thought I could do it. This was rather wounding to my pride, but of course they were completely right. The fact that they were surprised showed how much I had needed to change.

In November 2017, as I sat with Robin Weekes for one of our regular sessions, another prayer crystallised for me. I began to pray daily that 'each day I will be able to love, serve and care for Shoko in the best way for her'.

I prayed this prayer myself and asked others to pray it for me.

It reminded me of my priority for the day, to focus on Shoko and her needs. It wasn't about myself and my feelings (I already knew that), but thinking about Shoko and asking for the strength and grace I would need to care for her that day.

It was also important to take 'each day' at a time. I should not try to look further ahead. That only led to speculation and anxiety. It was Jesus who said, 'do not be anxious about tomorrow' (Matthew 6:34). And He was right.

I wrote to my sister:

> *23rd November 2017*
> *I can't/don't want to think about future days (how many? what will happen?) but just focus on this day, receiving it each morning as a gift and praying that we will have a good day, full of joy for both of us and of peace for Shoko, without anxiety or worry for her, right up to the end of the day. That helps me a lot and I need to stick to it.*

17
2018: Constant Love, Growing Confusion

The year 2018 began well and we were in a good routine, both day and night. Shoko was more and more affectionate, though sometimes the way she expressed it seemed confused. I found myself writing more in my journal, which to this point had been 'occasional':

14th January

We sat at table for supper and she wasn't eating very much. She kept offering me food from her plate and I kept pushing it back, because I was worried that she wouldn't eat. She burst into tears.

'You're rejecting me. If you just say thank you, I'll be so happy. I want to give you food to eat.'

I had forgotten how important my body language was. I was feeling concern (for her well-being? or worried about her sleep?) – but I was communicating annoyance.

I could only say sorry and take the plate with thanks. That made her happy, though she was still tearful. She didn't want to eat but wanted to go to bed. Then she said, 'I love you so much. Please eat whatever you want. It makes me happy.' Later upstairs she said again, 'I love you. I missed you so much.'

'Why are you crying?' I asked.

'Because I love you so much.'

15th January

This evening we sang 'I Will Sing the Wondrous Story'. [36] She read the words again with emphasis and was moved to tears.

27th January

'Someone keeps telling me that I'm doing bad things. They say I'm telling lies… please forgive me, I'm so sorry.'

'But you haven't done anything wrong,' I replied. 'You've done everything in the right way. Please don't worry about it.'

'Thank you. You are a very good person, Otōsan.'

28th January

The last two mornings I woke up dreaming about her. She was wearing a sweatshirt with the wind blowing through her hair, just like one of her earlier pictures.

I love her so much but I don't find it easy. Sometimes I feel very lonely. Our communication is loving but very limited.

---

[36] Francis Harold Rowley (1854–1952).

I need to take each day as it comes, thanking God for it and focusing on that day. This disease is horrible but at least good has come out of it, as our love increases.

By this time Shoko was no longer reading books. She could still read, though with more difficulty in English. She was always reading the street signs and advertising, sometimes stumbling over the words. Occasionally she would read out loud from a Japanese book, sometimes several pages. I was never sure how much she understood, as she might read the same lines several times over.

She would look through magazines and fashion catalogues, flicking the pages. When she looked through her cousin's book about her mother's family, she would read the titles of each chapter and look at the pictures. She knew that this was about a place and people that were familiar but she didn't think that it was her family, or recognise the once-familiar faces.

She had a collection of pictures and letters about *'Parr Sensei'*, the missionary who had befriended her as a child, and whom she had known so well. Some of the letters had been written by Shoko. Now she had totally forgotten who *Parr Sensei* was, and just flicked through the pages.

She still loved singing together, but she would just hum the tune, while I sang the words. She still knew all the tunes and picked them up as soon as I started the song.

This was a time of increasing lack of continence. It wasn't real incontinence, just more 'accidents', both in the day and at night.

Emotions could change very quickly.

28th January 2018

As Shoko was getting ready for bed, suddenly she looked at the big calendar picture of a dog, which she usually loved to see. 'This is very bad,' she said. Then as I tried to help her take her jacket off to get into bed she wasn't pleased and slapped me a couple of times. But after a few seconds she calmed down again. As we sat together she became relaxed.

I began to talk to her about how we met.

'I met you on the ship and I began to love you then, though I didn't realise it at the time. But really, I did love you. And then you came to see me in Madras and we got engaged. Then you came back after a few months and we got married.'

'Did I get married? Am I married? But I haven't told my family.'

'They know about it and are so happy.'

Increasingly she was thinking about her family in Japan and going to see them.

'How far is it to Tokyo? How do we go – by train or bus?'

'*Otōsan*, please come to my house. When you come I will give you…'

'I have to go but I will miss you so much, *Otōsan*. I love you so much and I cried…'

One evening as we were driving in the car, she said, 'I think we had better go the airport tomorrow, not now.'

'We are not going there now.'

'Oh, that's good, I thought you were taking me to the airport.'

The next evening it was: 'I have to get to Maebashi from Tokyo. But I'm not sure how to get the train. I feel quite lonely. I can see them calling me: "Come here and relax with us." But…'

But what? She couldn't explain.

'Don't worry,' I said. 'We'll think about it again in the morning.'

'That would be good. Thank you.'

She was very happy with Sarah when she came that weekend. She wasn't surprised to see her and was very relaxed. Sometimes she engaged with her to talk. At other times she was happy just to sit and look at her magazines.

5th February

At supper we had a confused conversation. Some people had been using the toilet, she told me. They had got angry with her, but she had been able to handle it and calm them down, so all was well. I praised her and told her there was no need to worry.

'Oh, that's amazing,' she said. 'I never knew that.'

She repeated the story and we went over it once more. And then again, and again, for thirty minutes. It was not negative and she was not upset. But finally I realised I needed to change the subject ('Divert!') and we did.

9th February

'They are telling me… my cousins… I want to go to Isesaki…'

As she went to bed she began to cry.

'Why are you crying?'

'I'm thinking of those people and I want to go and meet them… but then I prayed for them and I'm sure they'll be OK.'

She went on talking to herself in this way, as she lay in bed, for nearly thirty minutes, until finally she slept quite peacefully.

18
Going Back to Japan?

As Shoko went on thinking about going home to Japan, this began to affect our meals and sleep. In mid-February things suddenly changed. She didn't want to eat and she didn't want to go to bed. I tried to reassure her and persuade her that we couldn't go anywhere tonight. It was too late to travel. We could think about it in the morning.

15th February

We sat at the table but instead of eating she started moving her food from one plate to another. She wanted to get a box to put it in.

'I need to take this when we go. We have to go tonight. We're leaving.'

She went to the kitchen and was quite active, wanting to boil eggs, which we did. I tried to give her the usual pills to help her sleep, but she refused and was quite cross with me (I'm afraid it was mutual).

When we went upstairs she started looking in the cupboard, packing things in her scarf and tying them up in a bundle to take. 'We are going tonight.' She picked up two books. 'We'll take these as well... this is a good one to take, maybe this one. But now they are so heavy. I don't know whether we can manage them.'

She went to bed, then got up immediately and we went downstairs. Finally she settled back to bed, around 11pm.

Each night after that she would go to her bedroom cupboard to tidy the shelf, rearranging things, taking them out of bags and putting them into bags, taking things from one drawer and putting them in another drawer, sometimes rolling things up to try to pack them. Then she would put moisturising cream on her face and hands. Sometimes she put a lot on and needed to wipe it off with tissue. Then off to the toilet and back again, then into the bathroom to wash her face and hands, then back to the toilet once more. This routine could go on for quite a long time. She wasn't preparing for bed but just doing things, all the time thinking that soon she would 'go' – to Japan?

I needed to find ways to reassure her, keep her calm and help her not to think about going. I have never gone fishing, but I imagined it must be a similar experience. Like a fisherman waiting for the fish to come on the line, I waited for the right moment to help her to bed. Too soon and she wasn't ready. Too late and we might have missed the opportunity.

I tried to develop some kind of routine. I would give her the usual pills at the appointed time and hope she would take them. Sometimes we read from a Bible storybook. Occasionally she listened, but not always.

Then we would start singing some Japanese hymns. There were three or four that we sang each night, which she liked. Then I got her to sit on her bedroom chair and relax, perhaps put more cream on her face and hands. She might look at a book or play with a small toy dog. Then we prayed, and as she did so I hoped that she would become sleepy. Sometimes she did and I would help her to get into bed. Sometimes she would close her eyes and go to sleep at once. Other times I would sing her favourite song, 'Jesus Loves Me',[37] over and over again. Gradually she would drop off.

Suddenly it had become difficult for her to settle. We had been having good evenings and nights for several months. But now every second night was disturbed.

What should we do? Should we be thinking of some stronger medication? *Was* there any stronger medication?

As usual, I consulted Tim and Phil, and asked our GP to refer us again to the consultant. The consultant considered prescribing Memantine, a different type of drug treatment for Alzheimer's, which might have a calming effect, but decided it wasn't needed as Shoko was managing well in other ways. Our GP prescribed antihistamine tablets. When Shoko took these at supper time, it seemed to relax her a bit and help her to settle.

Things were slightly better, but I was struggling to look after her. I wanted to love her, serve and care for her, but I found it difficult. 'How long will this go on?' I thought to myself.

---

[37] Anna Bartlett Warner (1820–1915); Chorus, William Batchelder Bradbury (1816–68).

I wasn't taking the advice that Phil had given me about 'validation':

- Affirm the person's desire: yes, it would be good to go to Japan…

- Try to find the emotion behind it: what is making you want to go there these days? Obviously to see your family…

- Give reassurance: you will see them again soon; they will be fine; we can think of going tomorrow…

- Try to distract with some other activity: have a drink, peel an apple, sing some songs…

That wasn't easy. But as I prayed that 'today' I would love, serve and care for Shoko, I did find that I welcomed the opportunity to sit with her and talk to her, to sing together and reassure her. As we did this, she became less troubled.

> *26th March*
> *Today Jonathan came and we went to the airport to meet him. We also had two hours in the hospital in the morning, so a tiring day.*
> *At supper she didn't eat much (we had a late lunch). She was very happy to see Jonathan there, but confused about him – she called him 'my friend', or 'Otōsan' and asked him, 'Where is Okāsan (your mother)?' She also talked about going somewhere, so not at all relaxed. She said goodnight and went upstairs quite happily, though still not quite settled. But when she sat in the bedroom chair she felt*

comfortable. We sang a little and then I prayed. At the end I thought she had become sleepy but suddenly she prayed:

'Our heavenly Father,
As we look behind we see many good things.
Those who trust in Jesus, it goes well for them.
I have got behind in writing, but when I get home I want to write... writing is very good.'

... then a few sentences in Japanese...

'We pray in Jesus' name. Amen.'

It was a beautiful prayer. When she finished she got into bed and went straight to sleep.

31st March

As she lay in bed, half asleep, she began to talk. She was planning for the journey:

'I have to get the food ready to take, or we will be hungry...

'When we get there we will sit at the big table and all gather round...

Will we take the children with us? We have a dog – will the children be afraid?'

She went on talking – asleep? awake? – for about twenty minutes before she dropped off. This was Shoko as she used to be, thinking about food, planning and preparing the obento *(picnic) for her family and guests. It was completely coherent – a joy to listen to her. But of course it was the wrong time: just when I wanted her to sleep...*

14th April

She still talks about 'a man'... but she is less troubled about him. She feels he is more satisfied these days.

Tonight after supper she started talking about him. He wanted to eat, but somehow she refused him. He became angry and called her a fool ('bakayaro') but calmed down when she spoke to him kindly. So she was not troubled and told me the story quite cheerfully. She repeated it several times, talking for about fifteen minutes, speaking very clearly and emphatically. It was like her old manner of talking, with plenty of emphasis and familiar gestures.

Another evening she wrote a letter to him. It began:

Dear Mr Golden Slumber [this was the title of the book lying beside her bed]
We are missing...
PS we are seeing near grace place
PS Adela is coming and looking forward...
[Adela's name was on a piece of paper nearby]

Who was this 'man'? We will never know. Jonathan, who studied psychology, believed it was me she was thinking about. 'Her mood at those times depended on your mood,' he said. That part was certainly true, as I realised more and more.[38] But I still don't know who this 'man' was.

> 16th April
> Tonight she didn't settle to bed until after 11pm. At one point she was talking animatedly: 'I can see my friends in the classroom. They are chattering excitedly – they're going 'kya kya kya' [like the sound of a flock of birds].' She was obviously imagining them and perhaps wanting to join them.

All this time she showed me great affection.

'Otōsan ga dai suki. Chisai toki kara. Umareta toki kara.' ('I love you and I have loved you since I was a small child. I loved you since the time I was born.')

That wasn't literally accurate but profoundly true. The one whom I love now is the one I've always wanted to know and love from the beginning.

But emotions could change quickly again. When I became impatient with her, she said, 'Otōsan [referring to me] is such a strange person.'

When she didn't take her pills I would become tense and worried. Sometimes I tried to force her. That was never a good thing to do. She sensed it at once when I got impatient or cross.

'You are rough... you can go home... you can go away...'

---

[38] Lee-Fay Low, *Live and Laugh with Dementia*, p 78, makes the same point: 'people with dementia mirror the emotions of those around them.'

And she knew how to answer me. When I was changing her vest (which I had to pull over her head), she resisted as usual.

'Oh, come on, don't fight with me,' I said (kindly, I hoped).

'Who started it?' she replied.

Touché.

One day I asked, 'Why do you make a fuss sometimes about taking your pills?'

'It all depends on the person giving them.'

One evening she woke up after sleeping a few minutes. Now she was wide awake and not at all interested in sleeping. When I helped her back into bed, she got up immediately and didn't respond to what I was saying. Then, as I tried to persuade her, without success, that it was time to go to bed, she spoke to me kindly: 'Are you tired? Perhaps you are feeling disappointed?'

By this time I was so cross that I couldn't say a word. She wanted to leave the bedroom and go downstairs. As she did so she said to me very cheerfully, 'Excuse me,' and saluted. She was in a very jolly mood but I wasn't enjoying it at all. Finally, after some time, she settled back to bed.

> *21st April*
> *Sarah was with us and Shoko was in a jolly mood. After supper she began singing a popular Japanese song, clapping her hands and joking with Sarah. That night she went off to sleep very easily. But the next night she seemed confused and didn't eat well.*
>
> *'I have to go,' she said. She couldn't sleep and needed extra pills.*

I shared my feelings with Sarah the next morning: the nights were difficult because I never knew how it would turn out; sometimes easy, sometimes not. So I had to take each day as it came. But I told Sarah: 'You could see how strong and clear her real self is, through both the gaiety and the confusion. This is her real self and it will continue, beyond this life, I believe.'

The next day our old friends Kim and Cynthia visited, and Shoko enjoyed a lively singsong with them, calling her friend Cynthia 'Obāsan' ('Granny') very affectionately.

3rd May

I came back from the library and Shoko and Yuna were singing together and really enjoying it. Shoko was clapping her hands, then slapping her face, almost dancing. They were having such a good time: it was wonderful to watch. Then she saw me and stretched out her arms as usual and said, 'I love you so much. I love you so much.' I kissed her, while Yuna giggled, looking at us.

6th May

At supper she thanked me again for all the food and said, 'I missed you so much. I want to be with you. I love you so much.'

And she held out her arms to embrace me. Her love for me is constant and a great rebuke to my selfishness and lack of concern.

9th May

This afternoon Casey (our carer) phoned me at 4pm, just as I was coming back to the house. She couldn't find Shoko. She had gone to the loo and returned to find Shoko gone. While I searched the house again, Casey went outside and found Shoko sitting in our car (the car door had not been locked, fortunately). She told Casey she was waiting for me. I managed to get her back into the house and settled down by suggesting that we have tea together. Then we did go out in the car after that.

This was the first time Shoko had tried to go out on her own. We had heard about people's tendency to 'wander' but we hadn't experienced it. Until today. Now we needed to keep the front door locked.

We had reached another milestone.

19
Going Home

Things happened very quickly in the second half of May 2018. Shoko was on good form physically and emotionally and we began to add some short walks in the summer evenings.

On 13th May Shoko fell as she got out of bed at 3am to go to the loo. She cut her head on the corner of a table and there was blood everywhere. Miraculously, she was not in pain and in fact had no idea what had happened. We had to go to A&E to get the cut stitched. Our close friends and colleagues from India, Raju and Catherine, were in London that day, and Raju came with us to the hospital, which was such a help. Shoko bravely endured the waiting and the pain of getting the stitches and there were no further ill effects.

But it led to a significant change. We decided to move her back to her old bed in our bedroom (she had been sleeping in the spare room). It was lower and safer and she now liked it better. One night as I was singing to her 'Jesus Loves Me', she joined in the singing quite enthusiastically. She was enjoying it but it wasn't lulling her to sleep. I wasn't sure what to do and then she said to me, 'Thank you very much. That's enough singing. Why don't you lie down here beside me?'

I did that and she talked a bit longer, sang to herself, and then dropped off to sleep. I thought that was a much better way of doing things.

Two nights later she was again lying in bed and I lay beside her. She was talking, partly to me, partly to herself. She was imagining herself sitting with others. There was a man who was very kind to her (unlike the 'man' who had so often spoken roughly to her). They were eating together and she mentioned *'otōsan'* and *'okāsan'* ('father' and 'mother'), who were there as well. Then she said, 'They all said goodbye and went to sleep. It was very good.' She repeated, 'It was very good,' several times. She was very contented as she talked, for about twenty minutes. And then she went to sleep.

I was deeply moved by this. After all the weeks of being unsettled, wanting to go home, now she clearly felt that she *was* at home, in the old house in Maebashi.

I felt very happy as I listened.

Two days after that, we lay down together, talked and sang, and I said *'Oyasumi nasai'* ('Goodnight'). As she went to sleep, within a few minutes, I thought, 'This is it. We've found a good way to settle each night.'

I didn't know that it would be the last night.

The next day all seemed normal. Shoko had been breathless the previous day, but in the morning we went to physiotherapy as usual, then to Tesco, where she greeted one of our neighbours, Teresa, very warmly. We were both surprised, and pleased, at her affectionate greeting. After lunch I sat upstairs, wrote a letter and did some reading. We had a relaxed tea together, played with a little doll that Yuna had given her, and then went for a walk. At one point she turned to me and said, 'You have been very kind. You have looked after me so well. Thank you.'

I was taken aback.

'I haven't done anything,' I muttered in response. 'I wish I could have done more.'

Shoko was again breathless. We went home to sit down and she relaxed. We sang together as usual and then ate our supper. Afterwards she said, 'I'm tired. I want to lie down.'

We went upstairs and she collapsed and died on the spot, quite suddenly. The postmortem confirmed it was heart failure. It was a very peaceful death for her.

A few days later I learned that on the day before Shoko died, her older sister, Fusako, had a dream in which Shoko said to her, 'I'm home' ('*tadaima*').

I was shocked and amazed. My earlier relief that Shoko had finally felt 'at home' with her family was now reinforced from this second source.

For me there was another meaning as well.

Six weeks before Shoko died I had a dream in which I saw these words that Shoko had dictated to me: 'When I am gone, tell all my friends that I have gone to be with Jesus, as he promised. So don't cry for me. Read John 14:1-3.'

I wasn't expecting her to die, but I thought they were beautiful words and wrote them down in the morning.

At the funeral, Robin Weekes focused on 'going home'. He spoke about the two dreams and linked them to Jesus' promise in John 14:1-3: 'I am going to prepare a place for you … I will come back and take you to be with me' (NIV).

In those words from John's Gospel, Jesus promised His disciples that He would prepare a place for them, through His death on the cross, and take them to be with Him when they die.

Shoko was truly home.

Reflections

20
Holes in the System

'More than ever I am oppressed by the magnitude of the hole in the medical and care system,' wrote Sally Magnusson as she struggled to care for her mother.

> There are charities offering a chance to talk to other carers, little bits of support here and there, well intentioned leaflets and lots of websites, but there is no service pulling the medical and care side together in a way that is personal to you and to those of us responsible for you. This is the challenge that any new model of community support will have to address ... 'the empty centre' of dementia care.[39]

When I read this, I felt that we were in that 'empty centre'. Who would pull it together for us? But I also found people who are developing ways to fill the hole.

When we first received the diagnosis through our GP and the consultant at the Memory Clinic, they were kind,

---

[39] Magnusson, *Where Memories Go*, p 303.

professional and thorough. They were able to give medical information and to prescribe drugs that would possibly slow down the progress of Alzheimer's, though not of course reverse it.

They were always supportive, throughout the following years, especially regarding medication to help with sleep or pain control. We could not have had a better service in that regard. We could contact our GP's team, and when we needed to be referred again to the consultant, we had a visit from his psychiatric nurse and also spoke on the phone to the consultant. As far as medical care was concerned, we were well served.

But when we asked questions about managing daily life, they were not in a position to give that advice.[40] 'You can contact the Alzheimer's Society,' said our GP, when Shoko first received her diagnosis.

June Andrews writes realistically about the limits of what can be expected from your GP and the Memory Clinic.[41] There is also great variation across the country. Dr Simon Atkins, a former GP, points out that doctors have 'very little up their sleeves in the way of treatment' for any kind of dementia. So they need to refer you elsewhere for the important social needs.[42]

This is understandable. However, everybody agrees that the current division between medical and social care needs to be bridged. But how? And what social care is available?

---

[40] Mitchell, *Somebody I Used to Know*, pp 170-171, describes her similar experience.

[41] Andrews, *Dementia: The One-Stop Guide*, pp 249-254.

[42] Atkins, *First Steps to Living with Dementia*, p 69.

We went to the Alzheimer's Society, as advised. They were helpful, but in those early stages their help seemed less relevant and we didn't pursue it. Rightly or wrongly, we thought we could manage, and we did, for the first five years.

But when, rather suddenly, Shoko's situation changed and the burden of care fell on me, I didn't know where to turn. It seemed we were all alone. We went back to the Alzheimer's Society, by this time well established locally, serving as the 'Dementia Hub' for our local council. It became our starting point in discovering the wide, and sometimes confusing, range of services on offer.

We attended some of their drop-in groups, and it was also possible to talk to one of their staff when visiting the centre. That was definitely useful, though in the end it seemed to come down to 'the journey' which each of us has to follow. This would be in some ways different for each person and so, by implication, we would need to travel it alone. There didn't seem to be anybody available to walk us through, step by step. Perhaps that wasn't possible, I thought.

However, their support worker came to visit us to get our details and give advice. He gave very useful information about possible resources, such as the council's services, and financial matters. He also introduced us to a number of organisations working in this field.[43] It was good to see that they linked with each in complementary ways, as much as they could.

We started building up information and trying things out, as I have described earlier. We tried out our local Day Care Centre and other drop-in services. We greatly valued our carers and our physio. And we carefully explored the possibilities for respite care, residential care and live-in carers. We were also getting advice and support, of many different kinds, from family and friends (including my retired GP friend).

All this was extremely valuable. But it took a lot of time and effort. It seemed that we had to find our own way, at a time when so much was uncertain. Was there anybody who could guide us?

Among the introductions that our friend from the Alzheimer's Society gave us was a promise to link us with the community dementia nurse. As a result, I got a call from Phil Parker, who then came to see us, as I have already described. Phil headed the Merton Dementia and End-of-Life care team in a new project, based not at a hospital but at the local council, aiming to bring together medical and social care.

Phil was the answer to our search. He could give us a high level of professional *medical* care. He was able to advise us, and indeed to advise our GP, regarding possible medication, when Shoko had difficulty with sleeping. I could talk to him frankly about her prognosis

---

[43] They included Carers Support Merton (www.csmerton.org) and the Wimbledon Guild (www.wimbledonguild.co.uk). (Both accessed 8th October 2019.)

and what might lie ahead. He could link us to other services, organising extra rails on the staircase through the occupational therapy team, or arranging a visit from the continence service.

Along with this he offered *relational* care. He was personal, interested in Shoko, talking to her directly and singing with her, as well as listening to whatever I had to say and the questions that I was asking.

He was *accessible.* An email or phone call would always get a reply and often a visit at home. Phil registered Shoko in the new course on Cognitive Stimulation Therapy which he was running. He gave advice about carers, live-in care, incontinence and many other practical and personal questions that I had.

The team that Phil Parker headed with his two colleagues was a new project run by the Central London Community Healthcare NHS Trust (CLCH).[44] It was based within Merton Community Services – provided by the NHS and co-located with Merton Council. It was an attempt to bring together medical and social care to meet the needs of the approximately 2,000 people living in Merton thought to have a diagnosis of dementia. It was brilliant. But it was struggling all the time and hoping to avoid having its budget cut, when it needed to be expanded at least ten times to meet the need. This surely was the future of care for the elderly, not just for those with dementia, but especially for them.

Phil's help, and the different services that we were able to access, did fit together to fill the hole. So we were not

---

[44] www.clch.nhs.uk (accessed 8th October 2019).

alone. But there were times when it did feel very lonely and I wondered how to continue. At the end of the day (literally), I was the one helping Shoko to settle at night and to get through the day.

In similar situations, people constantly ask themselves what will happen in the future and how long it will all go on.[45]

We needed the support that would enable us to continue living at home and to maintain relationships of love and communication through the fog of Alzheimer's that enveloped us. We did receive it, but we wondered whether it was up to each family to find their own support network, or whether more could be done to enable them.

Was there a better way forward?

---

[45] Bernard Coope and Felicity Richards (editors), *ABC of Dementia* (Oxford: Wiley-Blackwell, 2007), p 23.

21
Finding the Way Forward

What is the way forward in serving the elderly in our society, and especially those with dementia, in order to support them and their families to live their lives in the best way possible?

My (very limited) experience is based on the personal situation that Shoko and I faced. There are many different situations.

Some persons living with dementia are able to manage well by themselves, particularly those with 'early onset' or 'young onset' dementia.[46] They are a significant minority.

Others do not have either family or friends to provide care. Even if they do, they may reach a point when the best care will be provided in a residential care home. There are many receiving excellent care in this way.

The majority of situations are like ours, where one or more family members or friends are the primary caregivers, doing their best to look after the person living

---

[46] For example, Wendy Mitchell.

with dementia. Exact numbers are difficult to come by, but it is estimated that there are 700,000 families in the UK that care for people with dementia. Their numbers are projected to increase by 60 per cent by 2030 and they provide an estimated £11.6bn worth of unpaid care.[47]

Each situation is different and the challenges are unique for each person and family. The suggestions that follow are based on what we experienced.

1. The person living with dementia and the person(s) caring for them both need support.

It is important to support the caregiver(s) so that they can support the person living with dementia, whether at home for as long as appropriate, or in residential care.

Our family felt that we wanted Shoko to live at home. And because of the team that was supporting us *both*, I was able to sustain caring and looking after Shoko. I was very fortunate: I had retired and was in good health. It was still a huge challenge. Many caregivers face bigger burdens that they struggle with. Many are caring twenty-four hours a day.[48]

---

[47] www.dementiacarers.org.uk/for-dementia-professionals/key-facts-figures/ (accessed 8th October 2019). Others estimate that in 2013 this was about 44 per cent of the total cost of dementia care. Social care was about £10bn and medical care about £4bn (www.lse.ac.uk/website-archive/newsAndMedia/newsArchives/2014/09/Dementia.aspx, accessed 8th October 2019).
[48] www.dementiacarers.org.uk/for-dementia-professionals/key-facts-figures/ (accessed 8th October 2019).

2. This support needs to be personal and relational, accessible and available, and professional.

This is the ideal, not always realised. We did experience much of it, particularly through the CLCH team led by Phil Parker, as I have already explained. What do these words mean?

Personal and relational
In practice this means:
- the support is based on your situation

- there is continuity of relationship

- the same people are relating to you and providing care.

Accessible and available
The best thing of all is to be able to speak directly to the person you would like to, either by telephone or email. That means a direct line or individual email address, if at all possible.

Going through reception or a switchboard is sometimes necessary. You can't always speak directly to the person you want to, and you may need to wait for them to call back. For example, the people in the continence service could not be expected to answer the phone, when they were out visiting people. So we could not get their direct numbers (though we could ask for them by name).

When there is a system of calling back, it's important that this does take place as soon as possible. We found that CLCH scored highly on this. Our GP's service also did well, on the whole. The limitation here was that it might be a different person who would call back. It could be difficult to receive a call from the doctor that one wanted to connect with. Sometimes they were not available, or they didn't come in on certain days.

The consultant and his psychiatric nurse were available, after we had been referred to them. The nurse came to visit and the consultant responded personally to requests to speak to him.

Professional

You are looking for contact with somebody who is fully qualified to provide medical as well as social care resources. They are able to give access to facilities, whether medical or other practical services. They should know exactly what is available and what to recommend.

We were fortunate to receive this kind of support, in all these ways. But I realised later that we had been *very* fortunate. Many do not receive it.

How do we develop teams that will provide continuity of care, that are related to the person, accessible and professional?

3. For this to happen, the system needs to change, from the highest level right down.

Everybody seems to agree on the importance of person-centred care.

> There is a clear and growing need for services which are available shortly after diagnosis and which focus expressly on helping someone to

carry on living independently in their own home.[49]

That implies teamwork and continuity of care, whether a person is at home, in residential care, or in hospital:

> In an ideal world there would be continued involvement ... from the team that knows them.[50]

> Continuity of care is paramount in dementia.[51]

Important professional bodies say the same thing. The Dementia Action Alliance's 'Call to Action'[52] and the Global Alzheimer's Disease Charter[53] set out ambitious goals for people living with dementia, emphasising the importance of enabling them to live well in the environment of family and community. That means providing the right kind of focused support for the primary caregivers.

John Killick points out that 'those with dementia and those who look after them form a partnership' with a strong interpersonal character. So the supporters have an important role to 'create the atmosphere in which [the

---

[49] Andrews, *Dementia: The One-Stop Guide*, p 127.

[50] Ibid, p 257.

[51] Ibid, p 30.

[52] www.dementiaaction.org.uk/assets/0001/1915/National_De mentia_Declaration_for_England.pdf (accessed 8th October 2019).

[53] www.alz.co.uk/global-charter (accessed 8th October 2019).

person with] dementia flourishes'.[54] But this also means that 'the supporter needs supporting too, right from the beginning'.[55]

So the priority for the 'professionals' must be, wherever possible, to provide a *dedicated team* to give *personally focused suppor*t to the primary caregiver(s), as well as to the person living with dementia, whether in their own home or in a residential care home.

This team will provide continuity and be accessible. It will integrate medical and social care. And it will be centred on the person – the person living with dementia and the person(s) providing their primary care.

It will work with the caregiver(s) and the person living with dementia to provide the most appropriate support from the range of services available. This could include carers, drop-in sessions, day care centres, music groups – whatever works for them. For us it was the carers who came to our home.

The idea of a team like this may seem to be common sense, even if a bit ideal. In fact, most professionals agree that this is the way forward. The National Institute for Health and Care Excellence (NICE), in its pathway for dementia management, states that each person living with dementia should have 'a single named health or social care professional who is responsible for coordinating their care'. And carers need support that is

---

[54] Killick, *Dementia Positive*, pp 17, 26.

[55] Ibid, p 42.

'designed to help them support people living with dementia'.[56]

The challenge is how to make this approach work. It cuts across existing structures and ways of working. Changing them will be a challenge.

For example, who will set up this team? There are different views.

Some advocate a personal care programme, delivered by a multidisciplinary team. They acknowledge that in practice this is difficult to achieve.[57]

Some suggest that the GP is best placed to coordinate such a team.[58] Others point out that there are great variations in what GP services can provide.[59]

From our personal, limited experience, it is not realistic to expect GPs to provide this service, especially as the pressures on them increase.

We definitely need a different model, with specialist teams set up for this purpose.

For us it was the CLCH team that fulfilled this. Phil Parker's dementia care team provided expert personal care and had links to other teams such as occupational health (extra stair rails), continence nurses (specialist advice and supply of materials), district nurses and end-of-life care (we didn't use the services of these two). They

[56] www.pathways.nice.org.uk/pathways/dementia (accessed 8th October2019).

[57] Julian Hughes, *Alzheimer's and Other Dementias (The Facts)* (Oxford: Oxford University Press, 2011), pp 98-99.

[58] Simon Atkins, *Dementia for Dummies* (Chichester: John Wiley & Sons, 2015), pp 86, 91-92.

[59] Andrews, *Dementia: The One-Stop Guide*, pp 249-51.

all worked out of the same office and we could access them all through Phil, or through a single point-of-access phone.

At a meeting organised for caregivers, two of us, independently, spoke of how much it had meant to have this single point of contact to such personal and competent help.

Another example of a team that works is 'My Care, My Way', pioneered by the West London Clinical Commissioning Group.[60] They have set up integrated teams that support the health and well-being of local people aged sixty-five and over. The teams bring together professionals from health, social care and voluntary organisations to work with 'patients' and their carers (where relevant), in order to help keep them well and plan together for any needs. Patients and carers have a single point of contact and individualised care.

The teams (health and social care combined) develop an in-depth understanding of the patients and their families and organise care around them, combining practical as well as health needs. They have built solid relationships of trust with the patients and carers. It is a model of long-term care, not just 'disease management'.

This approach is broader than dementia care but its way of operation means that it provides the personal, accessible and professional support for people living with dementia, and their carers, that we are advocating.

---

[60] www.mycaremyway.co.uk/ (accessed 8th October 2019).

How can teams like this be strengthened and expanded? There is no doubt in my mind that this is the way forward.

4. Whatever changes may (or may not) come in the system, you need to work now to build up your own support team.

This takes time and hard work. It was not enough for us to rely on the services of CLCH, excellent as they were. We also needed carers, friends, physiotherapists and others to help and support. We would have been completely lost without them. (We could also afford to pay for the care that we received, at least for a limited period.) But it took several months to build up our team: finding what was available, making contacts, asking friends, trying people out, discovering what worked.

It's also important to be *willing to receive* help and support. This is never easy, either for the person living with dementia or for the caregiver. But you can't carry the burden alone.

I was very grateful to Shona and Dick, who were the first to keep pressing me to build up a team. Without that I'm not sure whether I would have done it.

When do you start? I probably should have begun much sooner to build up a support team, before things became more difficult. I might have avoided the constant sense of crisis that seemed to envelop us. (But maybe it would have been as difficult in any case). On the other hand, some of the services that are now available were not around when we first received the diagnosis. For example, the Alzheimer's Society in our area considerably expanded its resources in the five years after that. Phil Parker's team didn't exist five years earlier. Many of the really helpful books that I have read recently were published within the previous five years.

But what is important from the beginning is having the *mindset* that you need to build up a support team. You are going to need increasing support, and the person living with Alzheimer's also needs to have people with whom they can relate with confidence and ease, so that when things do become more difficult they are there to provide that support. It won't just depend on one person, who could find themselves overwhelmed.[61]

Postscript: two further questions

1. Do we need the present range of different organisations offering complementary services? Would we do better to pull them together? Or would that restrict the choice and freedom that the different organisations give?

2. What about finance? We were not eligible for financial support from the council. We could afford to pay for care, at least for the limited period of eighteen months that we needed it (beyond that I don't know whether we could have). This was actually a relief, as it enabled us to get good quality care. Could we have done that through the local authority? The range of providers that they approved didn't appear to offer the same level of quality.

---

[61] Cutting, *Dementia: A Positive Response*, p 84, mentions the value of family, church, societies, clubs, exercise, dance and music clubs to provide further levels of support.

Of course, this was only our personal experience and so may not be accurate. But I wondered what service would be available for those who had to rely only on the local authority. Would they get the same person coming each time, or would it vary considerably?

Andrews comments that services tend to be low quality because the local authority has to tender and give the contract to the lowest bidder.[62]

There should be some way of providing quality services that all could access. Part of the solution may be a system of payment which will enable people to choose the provider that they want. This is already available in some areas. But there are no easy answers here.

---

[62] Andrews, *Dementia: The One-Stop Guide*, p 234.

22
Is Anybody Still There?

'It really is the long, long goodbye,' said Nancy Reagan as she cared for her husband.[63]

We all felt a sense of bereavement very early on.

'I say goodbye in my heart each time I come,' said Jonathan after one of his visits.

It was deeply sad. At the same time, I felt that this period gave me the opportunity to reflect on our life together, while Shoko was still there. It was an opportunity to think with *regret* and repentance about failures, *rejoice* over all that we had, and to enjoy the *resources* that Shoko had made for us to remember her by.

As I looked back, I could see a lot that I regretted. I wished I had learned Japanese properly from the beginning. We felt that we should use English at home, but I should have worked much harder to learn Japanese. I would have understood Shoko so much more and I might have been more sensitive, less impatient. I would

---

[63] www.cbsnews.com/news/the-reagans-long-goodbye/ (accessed 8th October 2019).

also have been able to connect more with her family. I looked back on our early years in India soon after we got married. 'Our mother was an adventurer,' said Sarah. Yes, but there were huge adjustments for her, to life with a new husband in a third culture, with which he was familiar. I could have done more to support her. Later, when Shoko faced difficulties from my mother, I was caught between, trying to hold both sides together. I should have been clearly on one side – Shoko's.

Shoko was not perfect, even in the rosy glow of retrospect. We had our ups and downs and conflicts, like any couple. We needed to forgive and be forgiven, on both sides.

But at this point I was most conscious of failures on my side. As I reviewed them and asked for forgiveness in my heart – I couldn't ask her directly by this stage – it cleared blocks and opened up our relationship much more deeply.

There was a great deal that I could rejoice over. I was constantly astonished that Shoko kept on expressing her love for me, especially in the last few weeks (of course, we didn't know that they were the last weeks).

I enjoyed her humour. One night I apologised to her for something: 'I'm sorry; I'm stupid.'

'Yes, you are a little bit stupid,' she replied. 'Joke!'

When she met our physio, Antonia, they made faces and jokes as they sang and played together. On several occasions I saw her singing, clapping her hands and laughing – with Yuna, Sarah, and once with Billy, our niece Tara's lovely new puppy.

I seized these moments and treasured them in my memory, grateful for each one.

> When you lose somebody to dementia, bit by
> bit, you can still put your hand out and touch
> them. They're still there. You can see them. It's
> a loss, but they're alive![64]

I was grateful too for resources that Shoko had created. Just three years earlier we 'discovered' the journal that she had written fifty years before. The book had been on our shelf all the time but neither of us had opened it for years. I found what she had written back in the 1950s, a young woman living in Tokyo, enjoying music, films and books. I couldn't read it but Shoko explained the entries and we enjoyed remembering them (she could still remember at that time). Then there were notes of her time of study in Chicago and London and the friends she visited in other European countries. I had known about them from the scrapbooks that Shoko had meticulously compiled, but the journal threw much more light on that time, leading up to the account of her journey back to Japan in 1966, and our first meeting on the ship. The last entries were about her visit to Madras in May 1968, when we got engaged.

It was all so vivid. I went back to the pages again and again, even after the time when Shoko was no longer able to translate them for me. She had also (more recently)

---

[64] Lucy Whitman, (editor), *Telling Tales About Dementia*
(London: Jessica Kingsley Publishers, 2010), p 116.

written an account of her childhood and recorded an oral version in English as well.

These resources were great when it was hard to remember what Shoko had once been. But they kept raising the big question that was constantly on our minds: where is the real self and how long does it last?

> It is 'like being on a long road, getting further and further away from myself', said Mamie Magnusson. But that is 'not the whole story,' her daughter wrote. 'My sisters and I are more intimately engaged with you now than at any time … We know you, better perhaps than we ever did, even as you know us less.'[65]

'She's no longer with us' but 'there is still something of her in her', wrote Erwin Mortier about his mother.[66]

So who or where is the real self?

This is, naturally, the subject of intense discussion, among doctors, scholars, philosophers – in fact among all of us, because we are all interested.

Tom Kitwood, the doctor who pioneered 'person-centred care' for people living with dementia, emphasises the importance of relationships. It is in relationship that a person remains.[67]

---

[65] Magnusson, *Where Memories Go*, p 211.

[66] Erwin Mortier, *Stammered Songbook* (London: Pushkin Press, 2015), p 68.

[67] Tom Kitwood, *Dementia Reconsidered: The Person Comes First* (Buckingham: Open University Press, 1997), quoted in Hughes, *Alzheimer's and Other Dementias*, p 102, and in John

Julian Hughes, a professor of old age psychiatry, discusses different ways that we can be conscious of our 'self', both on our own and when we relate to others and are stimulated by them. These continue even through dementia. He concludes that 'we can argue that our selfhood persists in dementia, even if our personalities change; often this is a function of those around us'.[68]

John Swinton, a theologian, points out that if the self is located only in the 'higher cortical functions' these functions do disappear as the disease progresses. A person may not be able to 'think' (as far as we can tell). Their capacity is certainly diminishing all the time. But is that their real self?[69]

Swinton also points out the fragmentation of a purely medical approach to dementia and to questions regarding the self.[70] The great strength of Western medicine is its ability to analyse and separate. That is also its great weakness. It tends not to take account of the whole person.

We are not just minds, nor is the higher cortical part of us all that is our self. We are also not just individuals; we live in relationship with others, as Kitwood and others pointed out. But what happens if people stop relating to us? Does the person cease to exist? One might think so

Swinton, *Dementia: Living in the Memories of God* (London: SCM Press, 2012, 2017), pp 71-86.

[68] Quoted in Hughes, *Alzheimer's and Other Dementias*, p 153.

[69] Swinton, *Dementia: Living in the Memories of God*, pp 63-65, 108-109.

[70] Ibid, pp 49-67.

from seeing those who are totally neglected and apparently unable to think or respond in any way.

Swinton argues that there is another dimension. As people made by God, he believes, we are held in God's memory. God does not let us go and therefore we continue to exist, even when we ourselves may have forgotten everything, including God. This sense of being held by God is also transmitted to us by God's people as they maintain relationships of love and care with us.[71]

These discussions may be confusing! As I tried to understand them, this seemed to be the bottom line: we are not forgotten, we have not gone.

Our self goes on living in relationship with others, and also – if we believe it – in relationship with God. And if God exists, we continue to live in that relationship, even when our mental and bodily functions fail, or come to an end in death. Robin Weekes, our vicar, had reminded me of Jesus' words: 'He is not God of the dead, but of the living' (Mark 12:27). I knew that Shoko believed that too, as she had told me in my vivid and surprising dream, a few weeks before she died.

Another way to understand the self is to think of the experience of love.

Wendy Mitchell speaks in a video to her daughters that she won't know their names one day but she is sure she will still feel the emotional connection of love. And even though she might not recognise her daughters, she would still love them.[72]

---

[71] Ibid, pp 193-198, 222-223.
[72] Mitchell, *Somebody I Used to Know*, p 138.

I experienced Shoko's love at every point in our relationship. Several years ago, before she became ill, when I was travelling to India for a short visit, she wrote, as she often did, a note to take with me, with words to this effect: 'I haven't been able to do much, but I have loved.'

The first part wasn't true at all but the second was so true. I remember on that flight missing her very much, but feeling very secure in her love.

When Sarah or Jonathan visited, Shoko was filled with joy, even if she was sometimes confused about them. She knew them and she loved them. Sometimes she remembered them after their visits and would cry, because 'I miss them so much'. More often, especially later, she would have forgotten within an hour. But the power of her love continued, whenever she saw them. At other times she would spontaneously mention 'Sarah' or 'Jonathan' or one of her sisters. She was conscious of them, *feeling* for them, however little it might have appeared.

On our last walk together, as I have mentioned, she turned to me quite unexpectedly and said, 'You have been very kind. You have looked after me so well. Thank you.' I was taken aback and muttered in response, 'I wish I could have done more.'

This was her real self, expressed in love.

I was privileged to see the evidence of her love right up to the end. Others have experienced a much deeper loss of personality and consciousness in those whom they love. They don't recognise them. They can't speak. They appear not to respond at all. That is so sad, almost impossible to bear.

Even then, it seems that there are ways of communicating, and evidence that the real self is still there. John Killick gives a number of examples from his interactions, and others have found the same. It takes love to find it.[73]

23
The Power of Love

What is the most important thing we can do for the person living with Alzheimer's, or other types of dementia? It is easy to feel powerless and uncomfortable. 'I don't go to visit my grandmother in her care home,' a young friend told me. 'I don't know how I can relate to her or help her.'

There are many practical things we can do. But what I learned – rather slowly, rather late in the day – was that my most significant contribution was the way I related to Shoko.

'Your body language is more important than what you say,' Sarah told me many times, long before I understood it myself.

It was true. If the tone of my voice was impatient, or if I hustled Shoko to sit down, or get up, or go out, she found it distressing. Sometimes it made her cry. 'Why are you so cross with me?' If I learned to speak softly, to hold out an encouraging hand, the rewarding smile warmed me out of all proportion.

Of course, maintaining that kind of relationship isn't automatic. There is a lot that we need to learn about how to listen and observe, how to distract and reassure rather than contradict, how to develop enjoyable activities. Jude Wilton comments: 'It all needs tolerance, creativity, stamina, a sense of humour and heaps of patience! It can be emotionally and physically exhausting... But it's not all doom and gloom: it is still possible to have fun and laughter.'[74]

That is the main thrust of Lee-Fay Low's book *Live and Laugh with Dementia*. By engaging in positive activities you are maintaining and strengthening the person with dementia's relationship abilities.[75] Activities provide mental and physical stimulation and are pleasurable. The experience of pleasure leads to continued good feeling, which contributes to our flourishing. Even if the person doesn't remember the pleasurable experiences, they have value.[76]

Active relationships also help to maintain a person's self-identity. For people with dementia, 'their lives are based on snapshots of "now" rather than being informed by past memories and future plans'. So they 'rely on ... the way they are treated by the people around them, to tell them who they are in the world and how things are ... If people round them treat them with respect and happiness they are more likely to feel like a respected and happy person.'[77]

Lee-Fay Low gives detailed guidance on how to build relationships and enjoyable, meaningful activities. There

---

[74] Wilton, *Can I Tell You About Dementia?*, p 8.
[75] Lee-Fay Low, *Live and Laugh With Dementia*, p 1.
[76] Ibid, p 5.
[77] Ibid, p 9.

are practical suggestions on developing and continuing conversation, introducing and modifying appropriate activities, for fun as well as for doing needed things around the house, encouraging reminiscence, engaging family and friends.

I discovered this book and skimmed through it on the day before Shoko died.

'This is really good,' I thought. 'What new activities can I find to occupy and stimulate her?'

I brought out a pack of cards to play a game in which you turn them over to find a matching pair. Shoko used to love this and had played it only a few months earlier, but this time she didn't get it at all and I put the cards away. What else could we do? The main activity we had left was singing, and fortunately we still enjoyed that each day.

I realised that Yuna had been doing a great deal to keep Shoko occupied and stimulated, as did the other friends who came each week. I was grateful for that. In a sense I could leave it to them, while I focused on providing practical, loving care, as best as I could. But it confirmed my realisation that this kind of ongoing relating to the person living with Alzheimer's is absolutely vital. There is so much that we can do, at all stages, and especially the earlier ones.

William Cutting's *Dementia: A Positive Response*, like Lee-Fay Low's book and several others, emphasises the value of a positive outlook, especially in the early stages, and gives creative suggestions for activities and ways of coping and communicating. When I looked back to the earlier years, when Shoko was beginning to have difficulty with memory and was worried so much about many things, I was often irritable and impatient. If I had understood better what was happening to Shoko and known some of the things that I learned later, would I have been less frustrated and more accepting?

Whatever the answer to that question, two things are undoubtedly true:

- there is absolutely no substitute for a loving relationship
- there are many practical ways in which we can interact with the person living with Alzheimer's, or other forms of dementia, which will enhance their lives and make a real difference.

While there may not be a cure, we can *treat* the person, not necessarily with medicine, but by the way in which we relate and help to improve the quality of their life. And slowing down the progress of the disease could make a significant difference, to them and to their caregivers.

That is all a great encouragement to persevere in loving care. But it isn't always easy, as I and every caregiver have discovered. And the primary caregiver(s) can't do this alone. They are the ones under constant pressure, sometimes discouraged despite their efforts. They need support. That is why they need to build their support team.

And that is why friends are so important, both for the person living with dementia and for caregivers.

However, friends don't always find it easy. They may come and find their old friend so changed, perhaps not recognising them. Or even if they recognise them, they may not engage very much with them that day. If that is all that the friends see, they may easily become discouraged and wonder if it is worthwhile to visit.

'Today Shoko sat very quietly, not doing much,' said Adela. 'It was quite sad to see.' But she kept visiting, and was brilliant at engaging her with music, pictures on her iPad and things to laugh about.

'I found it very hard,' said Kazuko. But she had come all the way from Japan and Shoko had recognised her sister. Their best time together was singing familiar Japanese songs, which Shoko could recall well.

Friends need to remember that the person might be quite different on another day. Even if they aren't, that's what friends are for. The visit could also be a great support to the caregiver. If friends stop visiting, as sometimes happens when the dementia continues over a long period, the caregiver(s) can become isolated and alone, especially if they have no other family.

Friends or relatives find it hard when a loved one is so changed. They may feel that they would rather remember them as they were before. They don't realise that they can still learn more about them, as they are now, as well as remembering how they were in their past.

Visiting isn't always possible. It might be a phone call, letter, email, video call – whatever works. A friend used to phone me regularly, just to ask how things were going. Others would email. Friends need to take the initiative and to keep going, even when visits may seem difficult. It is not a matter of technique, just friendliness and warmth.

A friend from India came to see us while he was in London. We had known him and his wife from the time that we got engaged in Madras, fifty years earlier. Shoko didn't remember him now but realised he was somebody close to us and welcomed him, though at times she was disengaged. I was amazed at the intuitive way in which Ken related to her, talking to her warmly and directly, not at all put off when she didn't respond.

Friends don't forget. They don't stay away. And they don't give up.

Social groups outside the home can play an important role too, so it is good to maintain them as far as possible, or to try new ones – for example, music, exercise, or drop-in groups organised by various charities. For Shoko, Sunday morning in church was a highlight, not just for the spiritual truth she might have gained but also for the sense of being with other people, listening to the music, watching the children and being greeted warmly by everybody we met. We should perhaps have worked at joining other social groups in the earlier period, when Shoko might have been better able to adapt and be more comfortable with people.

Even if the situation is very discouraging, as it can be, that is what friends and family are there for, to go on showing love and care, because their friends and relatives are still people worthy of love and respect. And it is very much through others that all of us have our sense of self-worth. We help each other to remember who we are.

I was deeply moved by a letter from Phil Parker. He wrote, 'You should be proud to have preserved Shoko's personhood, sense of identity and all that was important to her, even in the face of an illness that was trying to strip her of these things.'

I was all too aware of how little I had done. But I understood the profound truth about Shoko that he was communicating. Alzheimer's, and other forms of dementia, can be fearsome diseases, but our response need not be fearful.

> Perfect love casts out fear.
> *1 John 4:18*

Appendix
What I Wish I Had Known Sooner or Done Better

When we first received the diagnosis

It would have been good to have had more guidance: somebody to sit with us and talk us through:

- what was happening now

- what we could expect in the future

- how we could respond positively to both.

It's a temptation either to ignore what is happening and hope it will somehow go away, or to become very worried and fall into despair.

I did pick up information and guidance as time went by, but only after things had become quite difficult.

If we had been directed right at the beginning to the person who could have given us that talk and guidance, somebody with authority as well as a warm relationship (a person like Phil Parker, whom we met at a much later stage)… then perhaps:

1. Shoko and I would have talked more about what was happening to her and where it would lead. I still don't know how much she was aware – not very much, I am sure, but perhaps more than she or I acknowledged to each other. It wasn't easy. The very slow decline of the early years is deceptive. We probably wanted to know more, but also didn't want to know. But definitely it would have been good to have talked more together.

2. I would have realised that Alzheimer's is not just memory loss. It affects different aspects of the brain – cognitive, emotional and functional. So when Shoko became so anxious about losing things – a kind of paranoia – I would have recognised this and known how to respond better.

3. I would have read some of the books and other resources that I only came across much later. Below I have listed them in the order that (looking back) I would have found most useful. Reading them much earlier would have been really helpful.

4. I might have learned more about how to handle the different stages, and recognise which stage we had reached.

5. We would have worked sooner to build the support team that both of us needed so much as time went on – family, friends, social groups, various caregiving options. We were fortunate that we already had our close church connection, which proved vital.

So more guidance right at the beginning could have helped us do some things differently.

When Shoko became anxious or had difficulty sleeping

I wish I had realised, at all times, that the way I related to Shoko was much more important than anything I said. Sarah told me this many times: 'Your body language is more important than what you say.' So I needed to respond with love and affection, not irritation. When Shoko was so worried about things that were missing, I should have understood what was happening and not tried to argue with her. I should have remembered the advice: don't Disagree; instead, Distract and Divert. I did try, but sometimes it was easier said than done! I wish I had understood sooner the importance of validation, rather than argument, which Phil Parker taught me.

I did learn that when Shoko was having difficulty settling at night, my getting irritated was counterproductive. When I was able to stay calm and patient (which definitely wasn't all the time) it did make things easier, first for me, and because of that, for Shoko.

I wish I had been able to enable Shoko to do more when she wanted to help, particularly in the kitchen. I found that difficult, because when you are in the kitchen trying to prepare a meal it can be busy (especially for an inexperienced person like me), and somebody opening pans and turning the gas on or off at the wrong time is disconcerting.

I wish I had learned Japanese properly, many years earlier. It would have helped our communication at every level.

So looking back, plenty of room for improvement!

But there were some things that we did get right

Keep up with your friends
We worked hard to keep them informed and engaged, and continued to invite people home.

There was a period, in the thick of things, when this was more difficult and we did feel a bit isolated. I then consciously worked at keeping up the connections.

The other side of the coin is that friends kept up with us, for which we were grateful.

Work closely with your family
In fact, they were the ones who worked closely with us and supported us both at every turn.

Understand the power of music
We did a lot of singing, on our own and when friends came. It was one of the best ways for them to engage. Shoko loved it. And she was able to continue playing hymns on the piano.

Sort out financial and legal matters
Including lasting power of attorney, wills, sources of finance, etc.

Since I already handled most of these things it was relatively simple to do this – but it's important to have it done, especially if the person with the diagnosis has tended to handle these matters in the past.

Receive personal support
On top of the support from family and friends, I had deep and personal care from my two friends Tim and Robin. I could tell them everything. What a difference that made.

Take each day as it comes
Easier said than done… But a vital lesson which I had to keep relearning. For Shoko it had become part of her changed nature.

Remember the importance of love
Shoko reminded me of this every day by her love and affection, through all the things that perplexed and disturbed. She was deeply grounded and secure in God's love and her own loving nature.

Helpful Resources

Here are some of the books and other resources that I found most helpful. Below I have listed them, with brief comments, in the order that (looking back) I would have found most helpful. It's not a judgement on their value or importance, just the order in which they could have been most helpful to me. Of course, that is my personal perspective.

An overall perspective – the best introductions

John Zeisel, *I'm Still Here*, London: Piatkus, 2011

The person with Alzheimer's *is still the same person with whom we can relate*, but it is *a different relationship*. That is the main point of this warm and beautifully written book. It also gives a basic understanding of Alzheimer's and its main symptoms and their effects, together with detailed practical guidelines for communicating and building the new relationship.

This was the first book I read, at a time when I was struggling to understand what was happening. It was a revelation, giving a clear and sympathetic understanding of the person living with Alzheimer's.

John Dunlop, *Finding Grace in the Face of Dementia,* **Wheaton, IL: Crossway, 2017**

I read this book later than Zeisel but I would put it equal at the head of the list. It gives a clear and warm introduction to the medical facts, along with practical advice on how to relate and care. Dunlop's position as a geriatric physician gives authority to the medical part, while his experience caring for his own parents makes his practical advice compassionate and authentic.

Simon Atkins, *First Steps to Living with Dementia,* **Oxford: Lion Hudson, 2013**

Written by a GP, another clear and sympathetic overview, from medical facts to practical responses. Quite brief, so easy to assimilate!

Lee-Fay Low, *Live and Laugh with Dementia,* **Chatswood, NSW: Exisle Publishing, 2014**

This has a simple focus: how to maintain active relationships with the person living with dementia. It is extremely practical and full of optimism, with fascinating case studies of people at different stages of dementia, enabling you to assess what stage your situation has reached. I wish I had read this sooner.

Stephen Miller, *Communicating Across Dementia,* **London: Robinson, 2015**

This also has clear guidance on how to talk, listen, provide stimulation and give comfort to people living with dementia. The author covers almost all the relevant areas in a sensitive way, turning some of the key principles that other recent books advocate into simple and practical guidelines, with many examples.

William Cutting, *Dementia: A Positive Response*, Exeter: Onwards and Upwards, 2018

Good medical material with a lot of practical advice. It covers similar ground to the other introductions. Dr Cutting especially advocates a very positive and active response to the early stages, with the conviction that this will help people to lead a full and even comfortable life.

I read this book later than the others (it is a recent publication), so most of what it said was already familiar. Probably I would have found it helpful at an earlier stage.

Personal stories

Any of the books above gives a good starting point for understanding. Along with them it will be good to read these personal accounts.

Sally Magnusson, *Where Memories Go*, London: Two Roads, 2014

The story of her mother, Mamie, her gradual descent into Alzheimer's and the struggles of her children as they cared for her. The detailed accounts of their actual situation and the gaps in the system rang true to our experience. I kept nodding 'Yes, just like us' and was eager to learn what happened next.

Oliver James, *Contented Dementia*, London: Vermilion, 2009

This is based on the story of Penny Garton caring for her mother, but that is the starting point for a much wider exploration and definite guidelines for supporting people with dementia. It is a very particular approach. I found some of it less applicable, but the main thesis was really helpful: the person with dementia needs to be respected within their present world and frame of reference. So don't keep asking questions; learn from them; enter into their world. And always agree.

Robertson McQuilkin, *A Promise Kept*, Carol Stream, IL: Tyndale House Publishers, 1999

A remarkable story – quite short – of faithfulness and love, caring for his wife for twenty-five years. Very inspiring.

Jude Wilton, *Can I Tell You About Dementia? A Guide for Family, Friends and Carers*, London: Jessica Kingsley Publishers, 2013

This isn't really a story, but it comes through the words of 'Jack', a person living with dementia, describing his experience, which gives the basis for simple, practical and encouraging advice.

Wendy Mitchell, *Somebody I Used to Know*, London: Bloomsbury, 2019

The writer was diagnosed in 2014 as having young onset Alzheimer's, at the age of fifty-eight. She writes and speaks all over the country about her condition, giving a remarkable picture from the inside. Although she and others like her are a minority, the insights they give are really valuable for families and caregivers.

Lucy Whitman (editor), *Telling Tales About Dementia*, London: Jessica Kingsley Publishers, 2010
A collection of thirty stories by those caring for a parent, partner or friend with dementia. They reflect their experience of pain and loss, their struggles with finding support, and the hope and love that they also discovered. The whole book is moving and informative.

An overall perspective – more detailed and comprehensive

You might choose to begin with these books instead of the simpler introductions above.

Julian Hughes, *Alzheimer's and Other Dementias (The Facts)*, Oxford: Oxford University Press, 2011
Fairly short but remarkably detailed and authoritative, with good material on the personal and spiritual care of people with dementia.

The next two books go side by side:

June Andrews, *Dementia: The One-Stop Guide*, London: Profile Books, 2015
This is comprehensive, as its title suggests, covering the medical, social, practical, financial and legal aspects. That means that some parts are brief, but it's a reliable overall guide.

Simon Atkins, *Dementia for Dummies*, Chichester: John Wiley & Sons, 2015

This covers the same ground as June Andrews, as part of the '*for Dummies*' series. Although it is so comprehensive, I personally found Dr Simon Atkins' earlier and shorter introduction (*First Steps to Living with Dementia*, see above) simpler and clearer at several points.

There is a later edition of this book, published in the USA and somewhat modified for readers there. It is called *Alzheimer's & Dementia for Dummies*, Hoboken, NJ: John Wiley & Sons, 2016.

John Killick, *Dementia Positive*, Edinburgh: Luath Press Limited, 2014

The subtitle is 'A Handbook Based on Lived Experiences'. John Killick has worked with people with dementia and their carers for many years. He shares their experiences, often in their own words, to show creative ways in which we can understand and relate to people with dementia. It is accessible, practical and positive.

I read this last of all the books listed here and found it extremely helpful, perhaps because I had read the other books and it reinforced the direction in which my thinking and responses had gone.

Bernard Coope and Felicity Richards (editors), *ABC of Dementia*, Oxford: Wiley-Blackwell, 2007

This is written for doctors and other medical personnel, so it is quite technical in parts. It covers all areas, with strong sections on person-centred care and the use and limitations of medication.

John Swinton, *Dementia: Living in the Memories of God*, London: SCM Press, 2012, 2017
This is not an overview but a reflection on what it means to be a person in the context of a disease which takes away memory and threatens self-consciousness. Definitely not an introductory book but deep and ultimately very encouraging. It particularly brings out the importance of community and friendship to sustain relationships with those living with dementia.

Some more personal stories

Erwin Mortier, *Stammered Songbook*, London: Pushkin Press, 2015
Beautiful and haunting reflections by a writer as he watches his mother disappearing as a person. Not the first story you would want to read, but full of insight and love.

Robyn Hollingworth, *My Mad Dad*, London: Trapeze, 2018
Fresh and irreverent, as the title suggests. The writer goes home to help her mother care for her father, who has Alzheimer's, vividly described. Her mother dies first from cancer, followed soon after by her father. Her response to their deaths is deeply moving and actually the main focus of the book.

Steph Booth, *Married to Alzheimer's: A Life Less Ordinary With Tony Booth*, London: Penguin Random House, 2019
Tony Booth was a remarkable person and his wife, Steph, tells their story vividly. There are many helpful details

about how they responded to his diagnosis and the challenges they faced.

Lucy Whitman (editor), *People with Dementia Speak Out*, **London: Jessica Kingsley Publishers, 2016**
A collection of stories by people with dementia. A striking feature is the astonishing diversity, both of backgrounds in life and of the way the disease affects people. A significant number of contributors have 'young onset' or 'early onset' dementia.

Martin Slevin, *The Little Girl in the Radiator: A Personal Study of Alzheimer's Disease*, **Bloomington, IN: AuthorHouse, 2010**
The story of the author caring for his mother – highly amusing but also sad – as well as exploring issues of care and the central question of identity, as he discovers his mother's link with 'the little girl in the radiator'.

Jane Grierson, *Knickers in the Fridge*, **Morrisville, NC: Lulu, 2008**
Well written, amusing and warm-hearted. The author and her sister Sally were able to help their mother live on in her own home (Sally and family moved into caravans in her garden) and communicate using the 'habilitative' approach – very similar to *Contented Dementia*.

Jennifer Bute with Louise Morse, *Dementia From the Inside: A Doctor's Personal Journey of Hope*, **London: SPCK, 2018**
Jennifer Bute's experience of early onset dementia enables her to speak 'from the inside'; to show the many positive aspects, in contrast to common fears and stereotypes. As with Wendy Mitchell's book, her insights are valuable for caregivers and family too.

There are *many, many more* books, articles and other resources on every aspect of dementia. I have not included any of those that give advice on diet, exercise and lifestyle, nor those explaining research into the causes and possible cures, except this:

Joseph Jebelli, *In Pursuit of Memory*, **London: John Murray, 2017**
A brilliant survey exploring the many different avenues in the search for causes and cures for Alzheimer's, from Alois Alzheimer in 1906 right up to the present.

You will find many more references in the books listed above. And perhaps the most useful place to go for more information and support is the Alzheimer's Society: www.alzheimers.org.uk
Our local branch was very helpful.

Other useful websites

Age UK: www.ageuk.org.uk (look under information and advice/health and wellbeing/Conditions and illnesses/dementia)

Carers Trust: www.carers.org

Both of these were also very helpful locally.

Three more organisations to support caregivers

Carers UK: www.carersuk.org

Dementia Carers Count: www.dementiacarers.org.uk

Dementia UK (providing Admiral Nurses):
www.dementiauk.org